Keys, Codes and Modes

A Visual Approach to Understanding Music

Creators and Producer:
Designs in Communications
1187 Coast Village Rd #110
Santa Barbara, CA 93108

Publisher: Bookbaby.com

Brand Marketing:
www.axexel.com
support@axexel.com

Contact: support@axexel.com for purchasing information: quantity sales, orders for U.S. trade and educational bookstores, distribution and wholesalers.

Special discounts are available on quantity purchases by schools, libraries, corporations, associations, and others. For details, contact the publisher at the address above.

KEYS, CODES AND MODES - Volume I
First Edition - Printed in the United States of America

ISBN: 978-0-9797507-1-7 - E-Book
ISBN: 978-0-9797507-0-0 - Soft Cover
ISBN: 978-0-9797507-2-4 - Hard Cover

Library of Congress Control Number: 2020900021

Table of Contents

Dedication

This book is a labor of love and is dedicated to my mom, Elizabeth D. Ryan, who lived her life making the world a better place to be–through education–as a teacher, principal and inspired soul. She encouraged children and students to become themselves. She always listened and accepted everyone at the level where they were at the time. In addition, she believed in dignity, integrity and honesty. She stood up for those less fortunate and was interested in others as opposed to putting herself first.

"Music in the soul can be heard by the universe."
–Lao Tzu - 6th century BC

"Music is the universal language of mankind."
–Henry Wadsworth Longfellow (1807-1882)

Intention

The intention of this resource is to create a navigational guide for understanding music and playing the guitar. Graphic images and visuals depict constellations and reveal patterns found inside the world of music. Guitar players improve their skills through knowledge and the application of music-theory principles.

This method is designed to encourage, support and celebrate an individual's creative journey and one's personal search for self-expression. Familiarity and understanding bolster confidence needed to experiment, write, compose and play "one's own" songs. Improvisation opens the imagination. It expresses emotions and feelings through creativity, words, minds and bodies, souls and spirits.

This guide is created by and for musicians. This method provides an overview of music and supports teaching and learning efforts at all levels. It is designed for players of any age, level of dexterity and depth of understanding. This tool supports the professionals, singers/songwriters, "creative" types, students, teachers, music therapists, patients, hobbyists and enthusiasts. It reaches as far as one's desires are pursued toward musical realization, expression and style.

This guide provides references and resources. It is designed to be reviewed periodically, especially with questions, or when seeking a new direction and inspiration. It can be viewed sequentially and/or by interest. Images represent concepts such as: notes, intervals and inversions, fingering patterns, scales, modes, chords and progressions. Music, science, art–all are intertwined, interrelated, relational and conform to the universal laws of physics and nature.

Music opens the imagination to creativity, inspiration and expression. This guide helps to navigate music, in a visual and usable way. It is designed to expand one's knowledge of the basics and fuel a growing love and affection for music. With enjoyment in mind, this method suggests and encourages growth through one's dedication and passion. Frequency of practice and play are essential for development, growth and success in one's evolution of music and playing skills.

"The wonders of the music of the future will be of a higher and wider scale and will introduce many sounds that the human ear is now incapable of hearing. Among these new sounds will be the glorious music of angelic chorales. As men hear these they will cease to consider Angels as figments of their imagination."
–Mozart (1756-1791 BCE)

"I would teach children music, physics, and philosophy; but most importantly music, for the patterns in music and all the arts are the keys to learning."

–Plato (421-347 BCE)

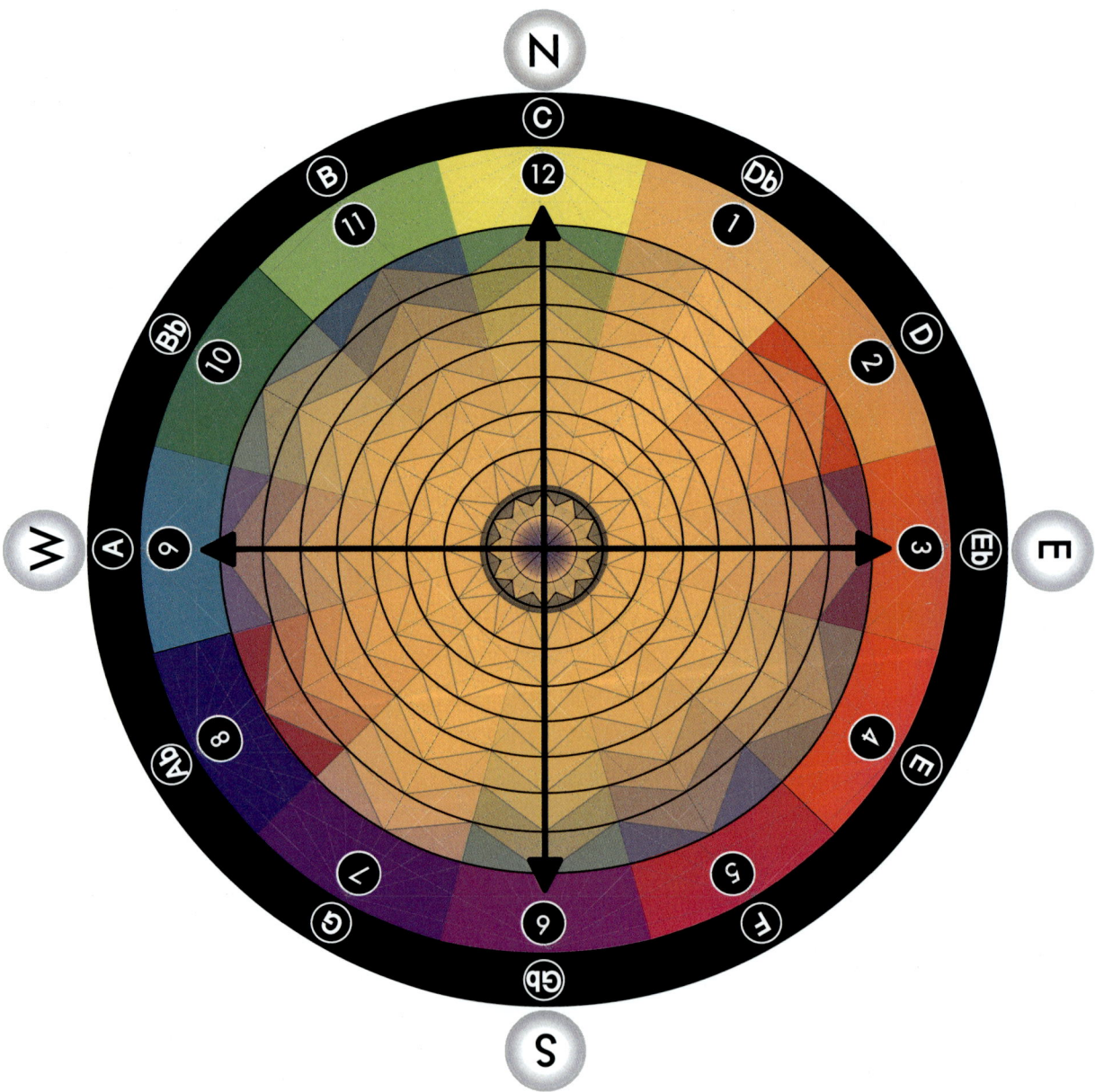

Fig. 1. This image represents a compass with musical keys, letters and numbers. This clockwise set of notes found on the circumference identifies the chromatic scale–all twelve notes used in western music. This is the "alphabet" of music.

Overview

Keys, Codes and Modes is a method which provides a viewpoint for understanding the inner workings of music. It is a starting place to explore constellations and patterns. Images and graphics act as guides to show how musical elements fit together. These images are used as tools for self-expression and the exploration of the how to play the guitar. The content is based on the primary elements found in music theory. This guide explores the foundations, as well as many extensions and extrapolations. It is a powerful tool to learn and understand how to improvise.

The Keys, Codes and Modes Method uses shapes, circles, compasses and the numbers on a clock face to express simply, the complicated concepts found in music. Images are used for the visualization and the demonstration of theory.

In Fig.1. On the previous page locate the C at the 12 o'clock position. The "Tonic" = "Key" = "Root" are interchangeable terms and describe the family of notes or the "HOME" starting place. Throughout this manual, C is used as the primary "go-to" and default key for most of the examples explored here. The reason for this choice is very simple; there are no flats or sharps in this key. In addition, it is perfectly relational to all other keys–learn one and realize how to transpose in all 12 keys.

The chromatic scale is composed of twelve notes. The major scale is composed of seven notes. These are two of the primary scale patterns, which provide an excellent foundation from which to play.

A note is a sound which is identified by a number, a letter, a position, and a function determined by where it fits in the scale. Each position in the scale is known as a "degree." This chromatic scale is comparable to the numbers found on a clock.

It gets simpler from here. Start with the big picture and choose which part of the whole musical concept to focus on and play. Most of the time, one reduces the chromatic scale to a seven or a five note scale. When the length of the scale is reduced from twelve–the number of degrees is lessened and is simplified. Calculations of functions will differ based on the length of the scale. It is simpler to play with fewer notes. Examples of shorter scales are: the pentatonic, the five note scale, C - D - E - G - A = (12 - 2 - 4 -7 - 9 o'clock positions) or the diatonic seven note scale C - D - E - F - G - A - B - C = (12 - 2 - 4 - 5 - 7 - 9 - 11 o'clock positions). Each scale will have a unique number of degrees, therefore, different ranges of scales to choose from and play.

A sharp (#) note is a half-step higher in pitch. A flat (b) note is a half-step lower in pitch. The A# and Bb can sound equivalent and like the same note. However, depending on the key and how it is used, they would be identified differently. In music, there are multiple ways of saying the same thing. The Diatonic Scale is often referred to as the Major Scale, the Do-Re-Mi Scale and the Ionian Mode. They all represent the same thing..

Another example of different ways to describe the same thing is known as an "Enharmonic Equivalent." An example is: C# = Db (C sharp = D flat), which are essentially the same sound, note or chord and considered to be equivalent. These will differ when the "same" note or sound is used in a different key or family. Which note/name to use is determined and defined by the key signature.

Fig. 1 on page 2 reveals likenesses to a compass; there are four primary points on the outside circumference, representing the directions: north - east - south - west.

As a clock, this image represents 12 numbers correlating to 12 notes, 12 placements, intervals and locations. The numbers on the face of this clock (1-12) correspond to the complete set of western notes–the chromatic scale. The letters/notes inside the parenthesis represent both: (1) "accidentals" - sharp (#) or flat (b), and (2) enharmonic equivalents.

C - (C# = Db) - D - (D#=Eb) - E - F - (F#=Gb) - G - (G#=Ab) - A - (A#=Bb) - B - C

This chromatic scale is the musical alphabet and the primary palette from which to choose one's desired notes to play. This is the complete set and range of notes found in western music. All other scales and chords are derivative(s) and are created from this original 12-note group. This chromatic scale consists of all notes, equidistant, measured in half-step increments, known as "semi-tones." This set of notes is expressed through different registers and octaves.

In Fig. 1, notice the 12 numbers on the outside circumference of the circle. The chromatic scale conforms to the correct order and spacing of these 12 notes names and numbers. These are displayed in an alphabetical, clockwise, positive and ascending order. These numbers are adjacent and correspond to the notes located in each "pie" slice. Information may be presented in either linear or concentric forms. When rotating clockwise to the right and to the next slice, the notes ascend and rise in pitch, one half-step at a time. When rotating counter-clockwise to the left to the next slice, the opposite is true; notes descend and are lowered in pitch, one half-step at a time.

Start with the C and rotate clockwise; each slice represents a half-step. It is the next higher note in the order of the chromatic scale. In this example, notes correspond to letters and numbers–"C through B" which corresponds to 12–11 positions of the clock. Each position is equivalent to one fret on the guitar neck.

The strings on the guitar are identified by the slices at the following positions: 4 - 9 - 2 - 7 - 11 and 4 o'clock. The note names and frets are referenced by the nut, with your choice of a string.

In this example, the strings are named and tuned to the following pitches/notes:

E - A - D - G - B - E

This sequence is known as "standard" tuning. These also correspond to the slice locations 4 - 9 - 2 - 7 - 11 - 4.

If one chooses the first or sixth string and plays up the neck–one fret at a time–one performs the E chromatic scale:

E - F - (F#=Gb) - G - (G#=Ab) - A - (A#=Bb) - B - C - (C# = Db) - D - (D#=Eb) - E

Using Fig. 1, follow the pattern on the outside circumference; start with the string choice/slice; then move completely around the circumference, one slice at a time. This reveals the note names and order for one's choice of the chromatic scales.

TIPs to be aware of, understand, know and use . . .

The "B - C" and "E - F" correlation. The notes "B and C" are adjacent and side by side. There is no "in between" accidental note–no flat or sharp (b or #) "in-between". The same is true for "E and F." There is no "in-between" accidental note. As a rule, there is no such thing as: B# or Cb and an Fb or E#. All other notes have "in-between" notes. Accidental notes are recognized with flat(s) or sharp(s) (b's or #'s) as identification. These are the black keys on the piano. Notice the 1, 3, 6, 8, 10 slices–each is an accidental, meaning it has a flat/(b) or sharp/(#) in its designation.

The 12 o'clock location is the "root," "key," the "tonic" and its central reference point–the Home. The C major scale consists of the following seven notes: C - D - E - F - G - A - B - C. These are found at the following locations around the face of a clock: 12, 02, 04, 05, 07, 09, 11 and 12 o'clock. These notes are referred to as

non-accidental notes, meaning this choice of notes has no flats or sharps. The points on the circle correspond to the 12 - 3 - 6 - 9 o'clock positions. These locations are important reference points for understanding and orientation. The 3 and 9 o'clock positions represent important **MINOR** notes.

Start at the 9 o'clock position A. This location identifies the A and the starting point for the **"A" relative minor scale.** There is an almost "identical" relationship between the C major and the A minor. They share the same notes. They share the same key signature (no sharps nor flats) and follow the same spacing pattern. The only difference is their starting points–the C starts on the 1; and the A starts on the 6. Notes in the "A" minor scale are composed of the following seven notes in this order: **A - B - C - D - E - F - G.** A is the sixth note of the C major scale. It equates to La - Ti - Do - Re - Mi - Fa - Sol. These locations are found at the following clock positions: **09, 11, 12, 02, 04, 05, 07**.

The 3 o'clock position identifies the minor third (m3) interval (Eb) in the key of C. To make a minor chord, simply lower the third degree a half-step. This note is used to form a C minor chord and scale. This results in a **natural, or parallel, minor scale**. This sequence is composed of the notes / spaces: **C - D - Eb - F - G - Ab - Bb - C.** These notes are found at the **12, 02, 03, 05, 07, 08, 10, 12** o'clock positions. There are additional minor scale patterns to study and learn–the melodic and harmonic.

Using the chromatic pattern with 12 notes, the 6 o'clock position is the halfway point on the circle and directly across from the C note. The 12 o'clock position represents the key (root) home. The 6 o'clock position is commonly referred to by any of the following descriptors: the flat fifth (the diminished fifth) or the #fourth (augmented fourth). This location is three whole steps from the 12 o'clock position, in either direction. This is known as a tritone–three whole steps.

Historically, this has been referred to as the Devil's Interval, due to its edgy, eerie, unsettling and dissonant sound. The importance of this note/chord is the need to resolve. It resides between a perfect fourth and a perfect fifth. Each is adjacent and a half-step on either side. It can be used to slide into the next chord. This note has been used extensively in Jazz, Bebop, Heavy Metal and the Blues.

Tuning the Guitar

"Everything in Life is Vibration"

–Albert Einstein (1879-1955)

Music is composed of elements, when organized, ordered and arranged, make pleasing sounds to our ears. Two basic and primary elements found in all music are: notes and rests = sounds and silence.

Notes are described in many ways and measured in both time and space, meaning duration and tonality. These are identified by horizontal axis (the length of time) and a vertical axis (the range of pitch from low to high) descriptors.

Tuning the Guitar - Standard

Throughout this manual, the guitar is in standard tuning. The orientation is based on a "right-handed" player's perspective. It is very important to keep the guitar in tune. An electronic tuner is one great way to achieve this task. Other options include: a tuning fork, a digital tuner, or a piano used to match tones. There is no "magic" like being in tune. It is a continuing effort to stay and play in tune. It is important to be tuned accurately in order to hear the pure overtones and the beautiful harmonics. Knowing how the guitar is tuned helps understand the relationships and interpret the intervals found on the fretboard.

Tuning The Guitar—*The Old-Fashioned Way* using the manual method helps one to understand the "physics" of the guitar, the underlying layout and the note patterns on the fretboard.

Start with the number-six string, which is your bass and wound "E" string. Turn the tuning pegs carefully and listen to the pitch fluctuate. Match the tone and frequency. Adjust the tension, until you match the note of E. Once you have the correct note, adhere to the following the tuning sequence.

Engage the string on the fifth (5th) fret; the resulting tone is the correct note of the next higher open string (with one exception).

Example: Engage the sixth string—E—on the fifth fret and the result is an A note. This gives one the reference note and tone for the fifth string at the open position the "nut". This interval on the fifth fret is known as a perfect fourth (4th). By doing the same thing again, engaging the fifth string—A—on the fifth (5th) fret, the resulting note is D. This gives you the reference tone for the open fourth string. Again, engage the fifth (5th) fret on the fourth string; G is the resulting note and the tone to match for the open third string.

THE EXCEPTION: Engage the third (3rd) G string on the fourth (4th) fret; B is the resulting note and the tone to match for the open second string.

Resume the regular tuning pattern: Engage the second string on the fifth (5th) fret. The resulting note is E, for the first E open string.

The **SPACE** between two notes and the **DIRECTION** of movement (up/down or down/up) are the two important considerations to identify whether two notes form an INTERVAL or an INVERSION. Intervals are composed of two notes that move in an upward direction (from a low note to a high note).

Intervals move in an upward direction.

On the guitar–moving from the bass (lower pitch) to the treble strings (higher pitch), the intervals between strings are all **fourths** (with one exception, mentioned previously, G to B–a Major Third.)

From the treble to the bass strings, the relationships are inversions, which are all **fifths** (except one: B to G, which is a minor sixth). Inversions are composed of two notes and move in a downward direction–from a high note to a low note.

Inversions move in a downward direction.

The names and numbers of the strings are listed below, ranging from the higher to the lower pitch.

~ treble to bass ~ unwound to wound ~

E (1st string) - B (2nd string) - G (3rd string) - D (4th string) - A (5th string) - E (6th string)

In the opposite direction, starting from the lower to the higher pitch.

~ bass to treble ~ wound to unwound ~

E (6th string) - A (5th string) - D (4th string) - G (3rd string) - B (2nd string) - E (1st string)

Ear Training is a valuable tool and of primary importance for all players. It can be very difficult in the beginning. However, it is essential to hear, feel and match vocally, tones, notes, intervals and scale patterns. PLAY and PRACTICE with CONSISTENCY and INTENTION. Play often with focus, frequency and commitment. Learn all the time. Push Yourself. Listen. FEEL. Music is cumulative and will grow exponentially with thought, practice, study and concentration. One way to accomplish this effort is to play an open string and match the tone—vocally—sing the pitch—name the note.

Move up one fret at a time and match the pitch, vocally—sing and name the note and repeat.

Continue this exercise on all twelve frets. You can do this on all six strings, one note and one interval at a time.

Another approach to practicing intervals is to pick an open string—match the pitch vocally—name the note. Then pick any fret and engage on the same string at the new location; hear the note, match it, feel it, sing it, name it. With practice you will soon become familiar with and feel all the intervals—the spaces between two notes. One "should" be able to sing intervals by heart or memory.

"Surely again, to heal men's wounds by music's spell."

–Euripides Medea (480-406 BCE)

The Guitar Neck - Fretboard

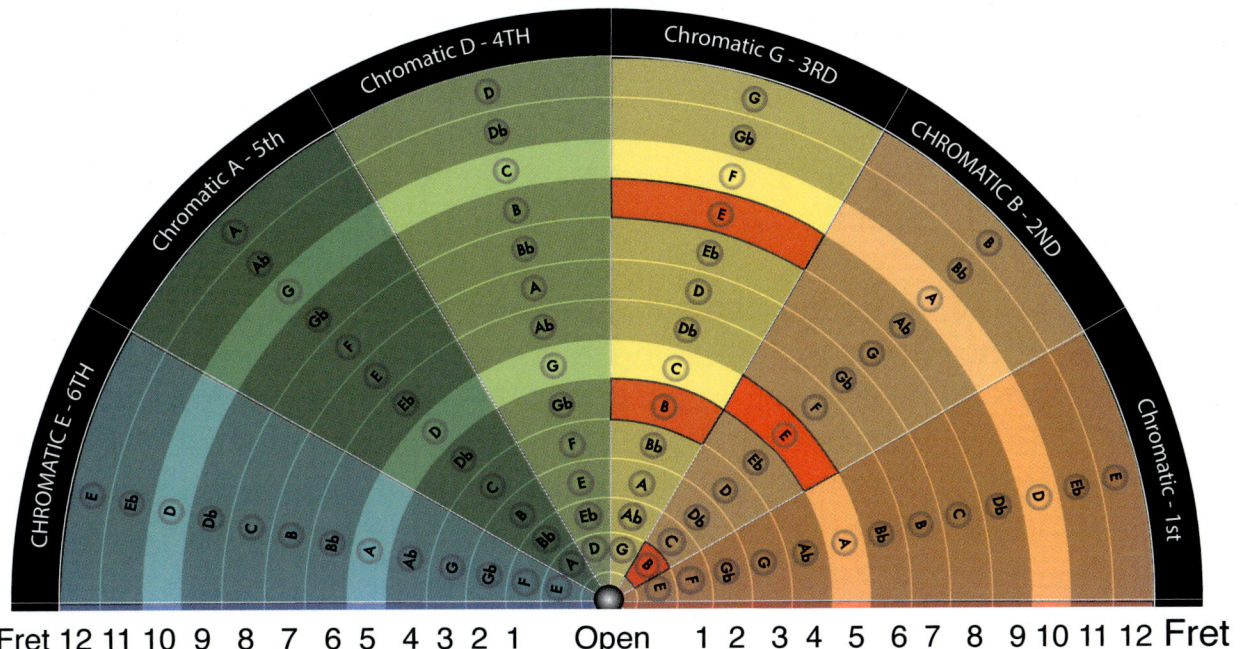

Fig. 2. The image above illustrates the six strings on the guitar. Each slice represents a string. The numbers below the image represent the fret number on the neck of the guitar. Each arc represents a half-step increment, a fret, string location and a corresponding note.

The blue slice on the left represents the bass, E/6th string. The dark green slice is the A/5th string, the light green is the D/4th string. The gold slice is the G/3rd string, the tan is the B/2nd string. The orange slice is the high E/1st string.

From the "OPEN" position, there are twelve rings radiating from the center. Each string, from the nut to the 12th fret, represents both the notes and frets used for the expression of the chromatic scale. The choice of string/note determines the key of the chromatic scale, as the naming is based on the starting point.

In the above image, locate "OPEN" as a starting point. Think of the innermost arc of notes as the "nut" of the guitar, or where the "open" strings reside.

Start with the slice on the left, which represents the bass–E string. Add one slice at a time in a clockwise direction; each slice adds one string at a time. Each wedge equals one of the six strings: (E - A - D - G - B - E). Each string incorporates the chromatic scale pattern and conforms to its exact order.

Each slice represents the notes on the string and the frets on the guitar neck. These ascend from the nut toward the body of the guitar. The outside circumference is the "octave." This is located at the 12th fret and close to the body of the guitar. It is also the "same" note class, and known as an octave.

Each concentric arc in any one slice equals one fret, a note, a half-step increment, a semi-tone. The notes in any one concentric circle or arc represent the six notes found in any one fret. The ascending chromatic scale begins with the letter name of the string, closest to the open nut position.

On the bass E (6) string wedge, the lighter tone in the fifth arc/ring indicates the letter A, which is the open position on the next (fifth) string –the interval is a fourth above. The lighter and larger ring/fret is the D, the tenth fret, the model or template note for the open note on the fourth string. This interval is also a fourth above the A (fifth string). You can see that notes repeat in specific patterns at different points throughout the neck. This offers insight to the layout of the fretboard, where notes are located and some of the recurring patterns.

The lighter concentric arcs are relative and share a fourth in common from left to right–moving clockwise, with the exception of the G (third) to B (second) strings–a major third. The red arcs of the slice indicate the one "aberration" in the tuning scheme–the interval between strings changes. Each string works the same, except G. That relationship changes to the fourth fret–a major third. The red note in the fourth slice provides the reference note for the B and second string.

When moving in the counterclockwise direction–from orange to green slices–from the higher pitched strings to the lower, these are relational and **inversions**–all fifths–except one–that relationship is the second string to the third string B–G, which is a minor sixth. These inversions and intervals are based on the direction they travel–intervals are up and inversions are down.

Fig. 3. Image provides the color-coded graphics as an alternative view of the six strings and the fretboard layout; see the similarities between the two. The following images represent the notes/letters and the interval names.

Notes and Intervals - Locations on the Fretboard

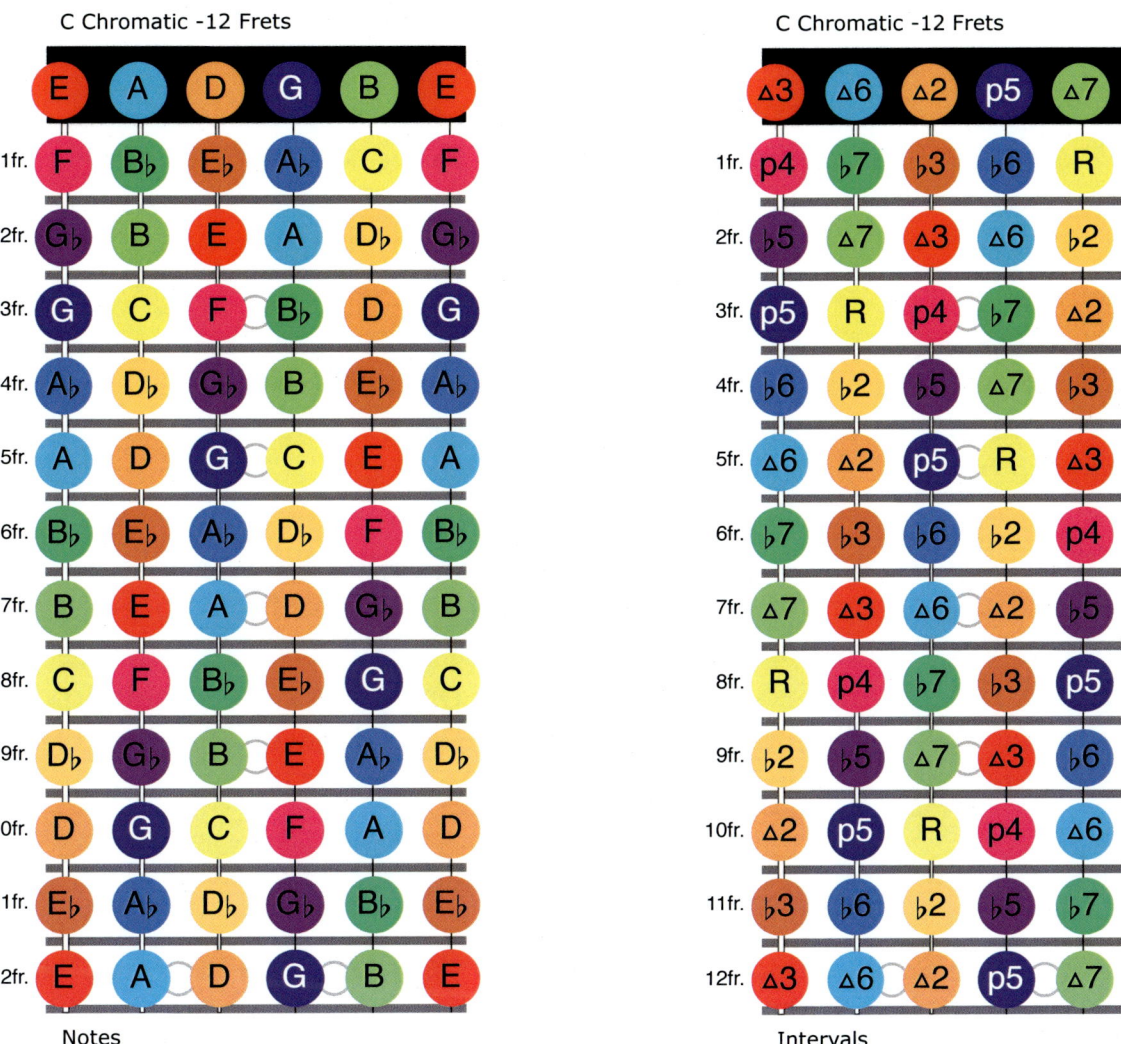

Fig. 3. These images represent the notes and intervals on the fretboard of the guitar. The key to understanding these two visuals is their orientation. The yellow circles signify the locations of the root in the key of C. The visual on the left reveals the notes; the visual on the right reveals the intervals–space between two notes. The top black bar represents the nut on the guitar neck–farthest point on the fretboard–away from the body of the guitar. The following explains the symbols: **"R" = Root, "P" = Perfect, the triangle "Δ" = Major and the "b" flat = Minor**.

The first column (string) on the left of each graphic is the lower pitch and wound E string. The sixth string is the bass and wound string. Both the high and the low strings are tuned to E and share the same chromatic scale. However, they reside in different registers. You can see how the pattern repeats–note for note, fret for fret and interval for interval through the color-coding.

The black bar on the top is the open-string position–the nut. Each fret represents a "half-step" tonal increment, which repeats itself every twelve frets. For best results memorize the note names, intervals and their locations. This provides powerful information to know, understand and use in playing, as well as composing.

These two images illustrate color-coded intervals found on the fretboard. In this example, the intervals are called out relationally to the key of C. C is in yellow and all intervals flows from C to their respective location(s) and intervals throughout the neck.

The high E is the first string and is positioned on the right side of each graphic. The low E is the sixth string, the bass, and is at the left side of each graphic. Each horizontal row represents a fret, which identifies the note names and interval relationships within the fret.

C is the "ONE," the key and Tonic. One location is on the second string, first fret. All interval relationships are relative to this reference point. In the previous visual, there are six yellow circles labeled with "C". Each location represents the C note and its octaves. These are interchangeable with one another–as they are of the same note class–just in different registers. When using the ONE, as the HOME or KEY, all intervals follow and are based on the number and degree of the scale.

In the image, each increment is identified with an interval name. The "C" circle is yellow and is the primary reference point. From the "C" all things flow: intervals, scale patterns and relationships to recognize, understand and use. Each interval uses a different color. This color-coding helps realize the spacings of intervals compared with their locations when transposing and changing keys. These are all relative, relational and interchangeable, including the number, letter, note name, interval value, color and positioning. This is a multi-functional guide as to where to locate it on the neck.

Each note corresponds to the choice of a string and the location on the fretboard. Each string starts with its own note name and ascends through the chromatic scale–fret by fret, note by note. Many of the "same" notes can be found in multiple locations on the guitar neck. The same note when played together or simultaneously is known as in "unison." Notes can be played simultaneously or sequentially. Two notes form an interval or an inversion, three notes form a chord (basic triad), four notes form an embellished/extended chord, or an arpeggio. Five to twelve notes form further extended and embellished chords, scales and modes.

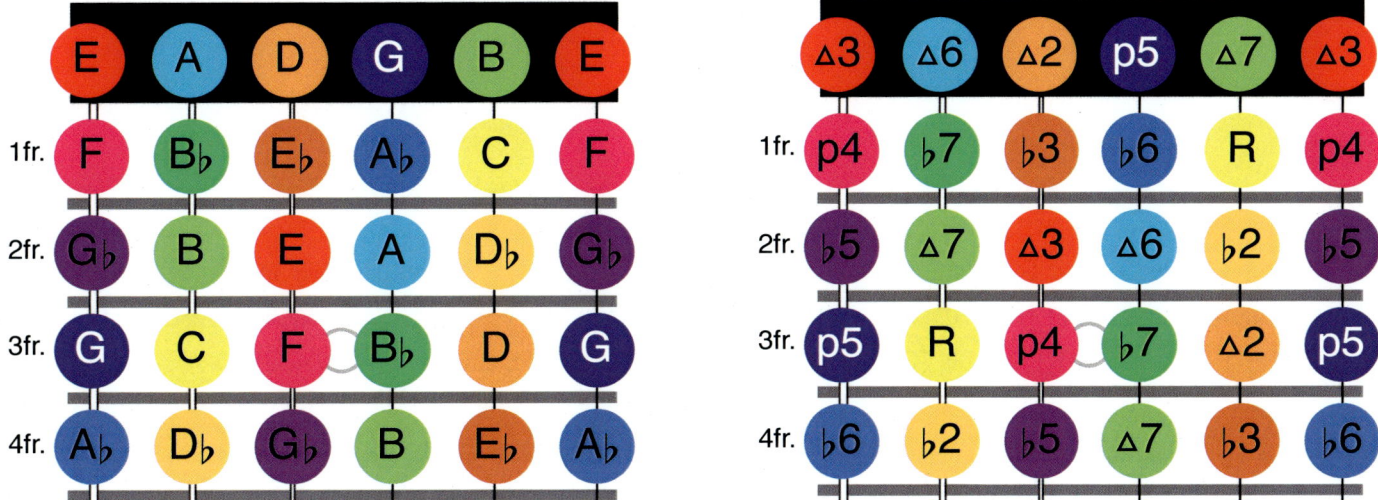

Fig. 4. Each of these images represents the nut and the first four frets of the guitar neck. They are identical except the one on the left provides the **notes** and their locations. The image on the right provides the **intervals**, the space between two notes, and their locations. The R or Root designates the Key of C–these intervals flow from C.

Notice: The F is the p4, or Perfect 4th, also the G is the p5 or, Perfect 5th. The nut is indicated by the underlying black bar, which represents the strings at the open position. The column on the left, starting with E and progressing to the F to Gb to G to Ab, are the first five notes of the E chromatic scale.

Use four fingers and plan to use one for each fret. Start in the upper left–hand corner, with the open E string. Move from the top fret to the bottom fret–one fret at a time and one finger at a time. Then move to the right–one column. Start at the top with the A and move one fret and use one finger for one fret, second finger for second fret, third finger for the third fret, etc. Continue with each column or string. One will have played all the possible notes available within the first four frets.

Notes

One note is a dot, a sphere, a globe—which varies in size, volume and dimension. A note is a sound, a frequency, a vibration, a point in space, a place in time. It is an essential building block found in musical structures and compositions.

Notes are blocks in time and levels in space. Notes occupy a vertical position on a musical staff (the x-axis), representing pitch, higher and lower tones. Notes also represent a horizontal space on the rhythmic timeline (the y-axis)—representing the length of sounds and/or periods of silence.

Sounds are expressed through frequencies—the number of vibrations per second. Any note represents an oscillation, a pulse, manifesting in a concentric or spiral pattern. Sounds and vibrations fill the air and the world. They impact our very thoughts, emotions and feelings. Every sound, object, body and belief has a distinct, identifiable and vibrational frequency. Each exhibits a unique signature existing and measurable in both nature and physics.

The note is the "primary" musical unit, the lowest common denominator in the musical hierarchy. All scales, intervals, modes, chords and progressions consist of notes. Notes are the sounds; rests are silence—each with exact time durations.

Notes are measured in spans of time and space. Notes are divided, split and fractionated into derivatives of time values, beginning with a whole note. Notes have different time values such as a whole, half, quarter, eighth, sixteenth, and thirty-second. These time values are usually in a pattern, either doubled or halved in duration. Each iteration is dependent on the direction and point of origin as to the result of its doubling or halving. As a rule, these values are even; however, it is possible to use triplets to add variety and spice—three equal notes in the space of one half note or two quarter notes.

Ordered patterns of notes, intervals, arpeggios, scales and modal sequences are used to express music. These groups are essential building blocks for creating fun, powerful and rich musical works. "Ranges," "Sets" and groupings of notes provide form and structure, with relational, relative and directional attributes. These sets and ordered groups are known as: "keys," "scales and chords" and "tonal families." All consist of notes, harmonic relationships and intervals. All music is interconnected and interrelated. Music manifests in waves, shapes and circular vibrational patterns.

Music is composed of notes expressing form in songs and compositions. A musical note has values, characteristics, functions and descriptors. These values include: pitch, the high or low level in tonality. The timbre is the quality and type of sound. The volume is the softness or loudness of the sound. The duration is the length of time. The accent equals the force. Sustain keeps the tone audible for extended periods of times. Attack and temperament are additional descriptors.

Pitch is determined by the number of vibrations per second. The higher the number of vibrations, the higher the pitch; the lower the number of vibrations, the lower the pitch. The size of the instrument also determines the pitch; bigger instruments have deeper and lower bass tones. Smaller instruments have higher tones.

Pythagoras determined the following: Double the length of a string–the resulting pitch is lowered, exactly twice as low. Shorten the length to half and the pitch becomes exactly twice as high. These resulting notes are known as octaves. The longer the string–the lower the pitch; the shorter the string–the higher the pitch. This relationship is inverse. A mathematical equation expresses it this way: $1 \times 2 = 2$ (2/1) or $1 \div 2 = 1/2$. Either way, these are the inverse of each other, two over one or one over two, doubled or halved.

The pitch represents the same note class in multiples of two(s) or halves. The result is known as an OCTAVE–the same note class found in multiple registers (higher and lower groups). Twice and/or half the frequency always result in octaves–the same note class. An octave is the note on each end on a scale; a bookend, it repeats in both directions.

The following diagram illustrates the octave with its relational aspects. Notice the three waves representing three notes and their relationship to one another. The red wave is the keynote and the lowest tone as indicated with the largest wave pattern, while the orange has twice the number of waves and the yellow has twice again as many. These are all the same note–located in different registers.

"The octave formed a circle and gave our noble earth its form."

–Pythagoras (569-475 BCE)

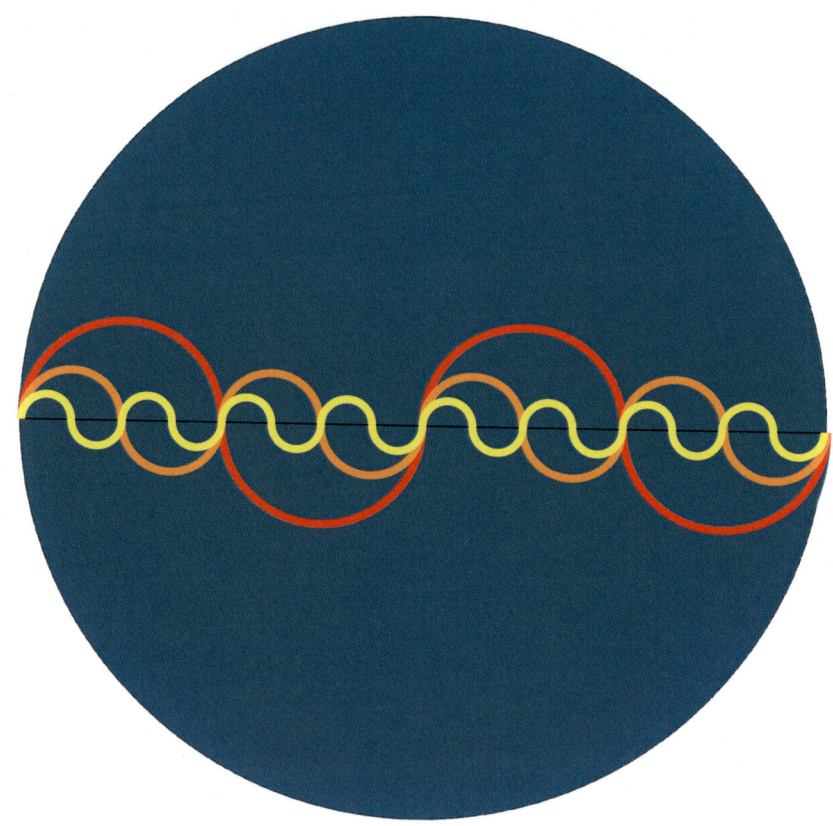

A musical composition can be compared to a jigsaw puzzle. Each puzzle piece is a note, and it fits in a unique location. Many small pieces form the whole concept, effect, or feeling. The whole is greater than the sum of the parts. One builds music with the first step; start with one note and a beat, and move into a complete composition. Take an idea or sketch and bring it into fruition.

Wavelengths, energy and music transcend and move through atomic and sub-atomic levels. These wavelengths are the vessels for carrying sound energy. The body/mind/spirit respond to music. As a musician, one is both the transmitter and the recipient of musical expressions and experiences. Infinite possibilities exist for creativity an expressive interpretations.

Impulses are the catalyst for the creation of rhythmic patterns, melodic explorations and expressions. Musical notes exist in space and time. They are charged with emotion, rotation, speed and momentum. They embed functionality, direction, inter-action, reflection and correlation to other points found in music, nature and physics. These are described by numbers, functions, letters and notes. There is "symmetry" within music, especially visible in augmented and diminished scales and chords. Letters form words, which form sentences and express ideas. A note is equivalent to a letter in the language of music; just as a vowel or a consonant, it is described by a sound, a letter, a name or a function. Music begins with a thought and a note, referenced by and relative to a particular point of view, as in a key or a genre. Musical works start with a note and have an ending point. Each is a journey. Musicians and composers use direction–movement–sway and swing–forward and backward, up and down, side to side and all around. Musicians use motion, speed, rate and time (i.e., when to rest, when to engage) to express emotion and feelings.

"Art is a step from what is obvious and well-known toward what is arcane and concealed."

–Kahlil Gibran (1883-1931)

12 Notes of the Chromatic Scale

Fig. 5. 12 Notes of the chromatic scale.
1.) Start with the C at the 12 o'clock position and move clockwise to any point around the circumference; the notes ascend through the chromatic scale and are identified in each white circle. 2.) Find the "C" note at the center of the yellow circle, ascend up the slice, incrementally, and one sees the notes that compose the chromatic scale. Notice they are identical in name and order to the outside circles; this is a great cross-referencing tool. Also, start at the 12 o'clock position and descend the chromatic scale one step at a time through the colored arches.

The Constellation of the 12 Chromatic Scales

Fig. 6. This image illustrates all twelve of the chromatic scales—within each slice and each concentric circle. This graphic conforms to the directional attributes. **CLOCKWISE** rotation **ASCENDS** (i.e., goes higher) through all the notes of the chromatic scale (starting with C and ending with B). A **COUNTERCLOCKWISE** rotation **DESCENDS** (i.e., goes lower) through all the notes of the chromatic scale (starting with C and ending with C#/Db). The outside note on the circumference is the KEY of each slice. It is also the beginning and ending note. When rotating in a clockwise direction, each slice and arc represents the next ascending note.

Within each concentric circle, there is a chromatic scale. Everything inside any one concentric circle is relational by position. They share "like" characteristics and functions with all the other keys. The "functions" of intervals remain consistent through all the slices and in all the keys. The notes in the chromatic scale are found in each slice and in each concentric ring–forming a matrix.

This whole pie represents the musical constellation of western music. Each slice within the pie is arranged in the chromatic order. It is relational and relative to the other slices and their respective arcs.

This pie is composed of twelve concentric circles, each represents a chromatic scale. There are twelve slices in the pie with twelve notes in each slice. Each slice represents a chromatic scale–a linear ordering of the notes. These data points may be viewed in either linear or concentric patterns.

The scale starts from either the center point of the circle within a slice or from the outside circumference toward the center, using internal arches as steps. The content in each slice is bidirectional. To ascend the scale, start at the innermost ring and move toward the outside. To descend, start from the outside ring and move toward the center within the slice.

"Do you know that our soul is composed of harmony?"

–Leonardo da Vinci (1452-1519)

Start at the 12 o'clock position, R = Root, rotate to the 1 o'clock position, labeled m2. This note is halfway between C and D (12 and 2 o'clock). The distance from C to Db is a HALF step, a semi-tone; m2 stands for minor second, as compared to a WHOLE step, which is two semi-tones a Major Second measured from the root.

Sharp is a half-step higher in pitch. "Flat" (b) is the opposite, a half-step lower than a given note (D to Db). Accidentals are three symbols describing flatted, sharped and naturalized notes.

Fig. 7. This image references the root, the note names and intervals—all color-coded with yellow as the starting point. Notice the numbers arranged in the same order as on the face of a clock.

Throughout this book, C is the key, YELLOW represents the KEY, ROOT or TONIC. Notice the circles forming a rainbow of colors: these represent intervals.

The outside ellipses near the circumference identify the names of the intervals: **(R = Root, m2 = minor 2, Ma2 = Major 2, m3 = minor 3, Ma3 = Major 3, P4 = Perfect 4, #4/b5 = flat 5, P5 = Perfect 5, m6 = minor 6, Ma6 = Major 6, Dom7 = Dominant 7, Ma7 = Major 7, Root-Octave.** These intervals correlate to the 12 notes of the chromatic scale. The ellipses found in the concentric circle second from the circumference reveal the names of the notes.

Intervals

Fig. 8. This image references the location and names of intervals. Notice the space and distance between two notes–measured from the root position. Start at the 12 o'clock position and rotate in a clockwise direction. Move to any point on the circumference; each distance is unique, which fits into one of three categories: Major, minor or Perfect intervals.

Fig. 9. Inversions are identified in white circles on the circumference of the circle. Notice the different design on each of these two graphics with respect to the white lines: the left diagram starts clockwise from the ROOT position–up the scale. The diagram on the right when rotating counter clockwise descends, and one can see the relational aspects of the circular display as compared to the linear.

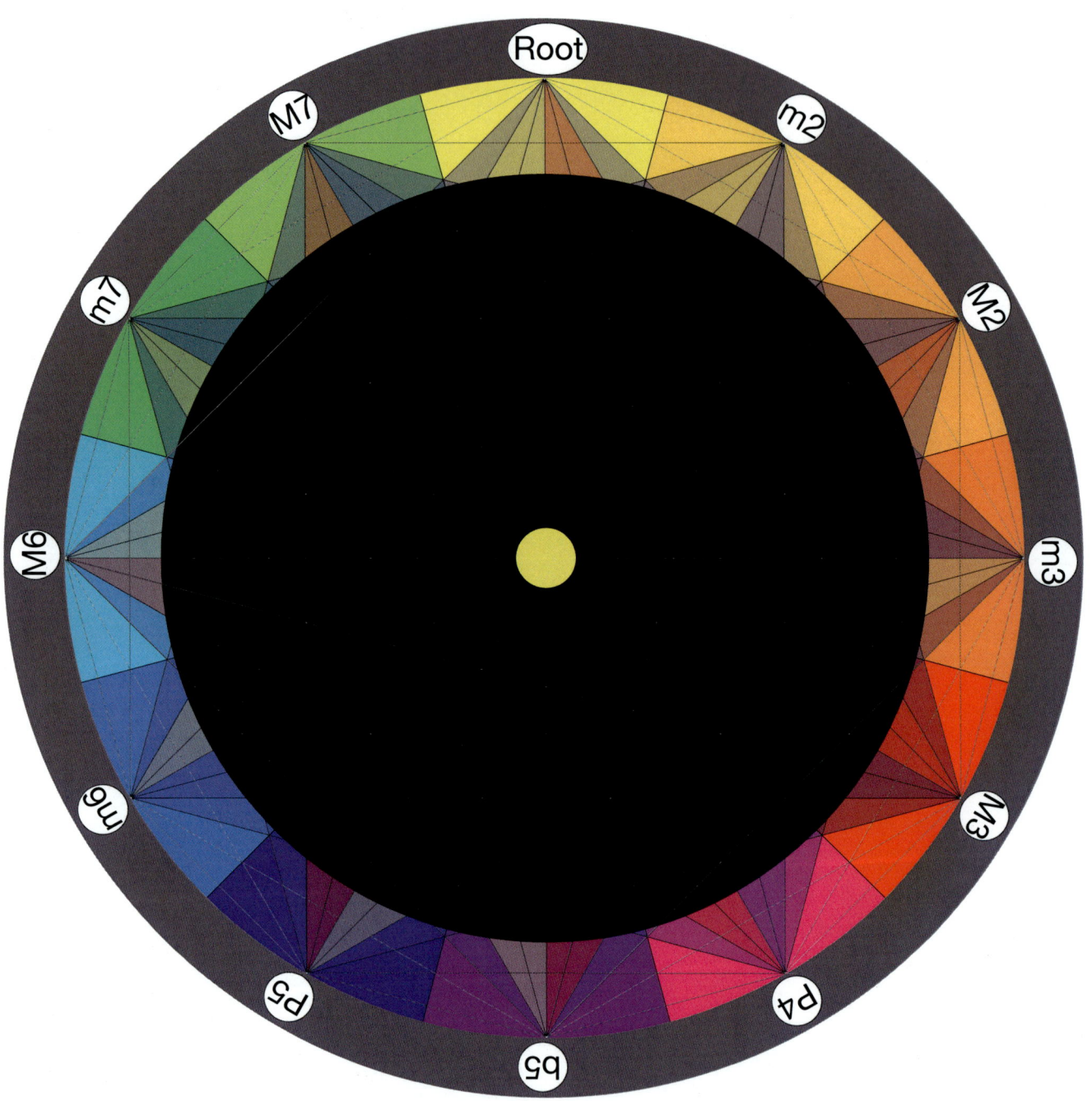

Fig 10. In the above illustration, rotate clockwise: the distances and points on the circumference reveal intervals. In a counterclockwise direction, the distances and points reveal inversions.

There are two types of intervals: harmonic and melodic. Harmonic represents a frozen or a static point in time, playing the two notes–simultaneously. Melodic intervals are played sequentially and fill a span or range in time.

Notice how all are geometrically aligned, relational and interconnected.

Inversions

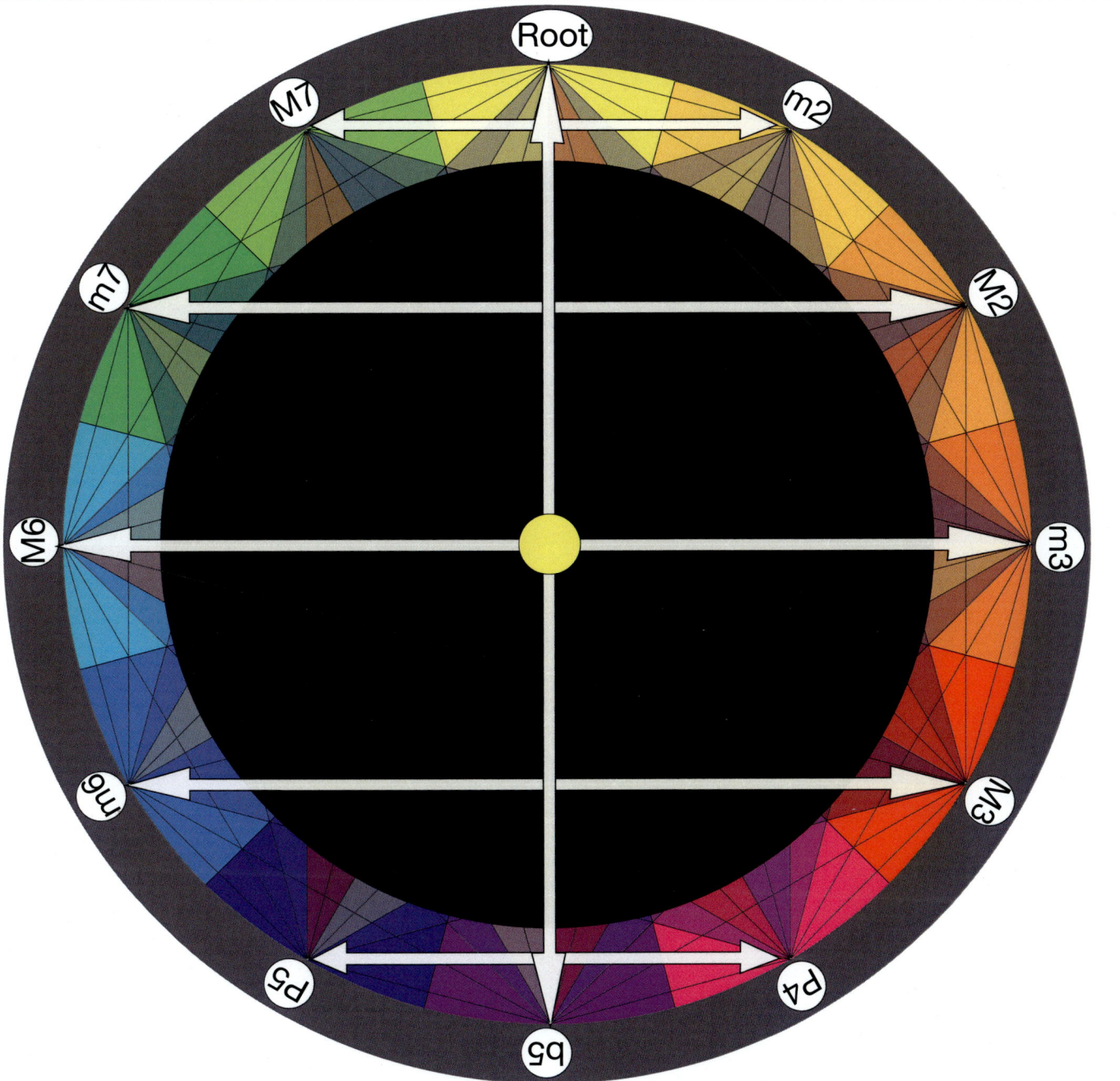

Fig. 11. Intervals–Spatial Relationships. Like intervals, inversions are the distance between two notes. However, inversions are measured from the upper note to the lower note–in a downward direction. Intervals and inversions are defined by the same two notes and are differentiated by direction, bottom/up or top/down. The horizontal lines are defined by endpoints–the arrowheads–which point to the inversions of each other. They represent the same distance from the root. The top horizontal line points to both a minor second and a major 7th. Both are one-half step from the root, one above–one below–each is the inversion of the other. The same horizontal line endpoints are equidistant from the 12 o'clock root position.

Wheel of Intervals and Inversions

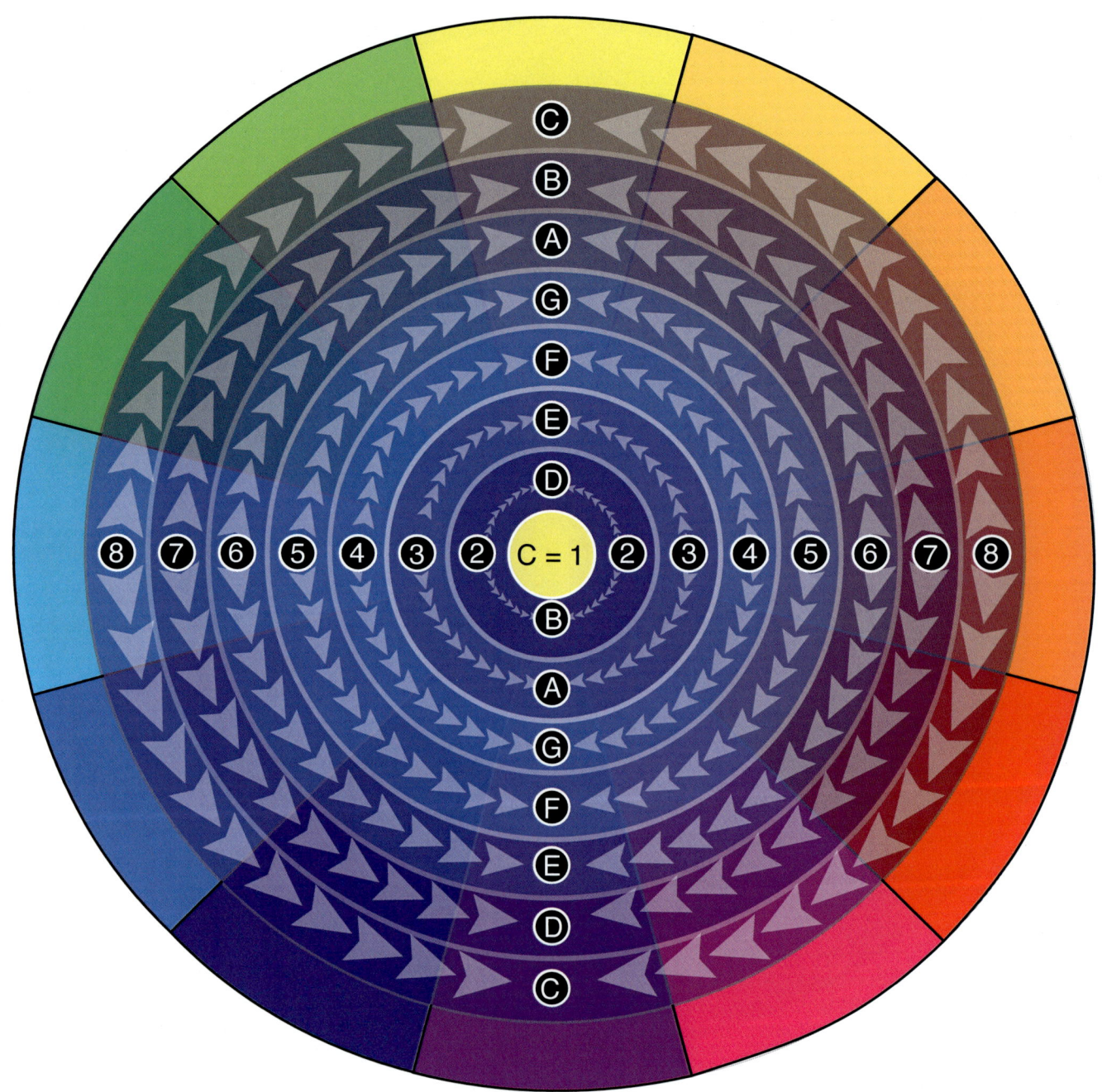

Fig. 12. The concentric circles (tree rings) are numbered incrementally on the horizon line, increasing from the center—outward—on both the left and the right sides.

The vertical line is a continuum composed of the repeating major scale pattern. The major scale is repeated on the vertical axis. The center circle is C; it is the "one," "root" and "tonic."

Above the horizontal center line, moving vertically, up on the X axis, and find the letters of the major scale in an ascending order. Each ring is a circle, an interval, and individually labeled: C - D - E - F - G - A - B - C.

Starting at the horizontal center line, moving vertically down on the X axis, are the letters of the major scale in the descending order. Notice the different order when descending down the scale: C - B - A - G - F - E - D - C.

How to decipher the example: From the center point, count to the right five rings. Follow the arrows up the circle in the counterclockwise direction. One reaches G. This provides a cross-reference point. The G is in the fifth circle above the C–the fifth interval in the major scale (C-D-E-F-G = 1-2-3-4-5). It is the fifth degree, or fifth point, on the scale. Any circle number when employing the counterclockwise direction will reveal the correct reference note. The concentric circle is interchangeable in this context. If one has the number, one can obtain the letter and vice versa.

The inversions reside below the horizontal line. They are the opposite, a reflection, a mirror image, the reciprocal, the flip side of an interval–from top to bottom. Example: To determine an inversion: count out from the center, to the right to circle five, follow the arrows down and in a clockwise direction to F. Yes, it is the same circle as the earlier example, However, based on the direction, things change. This time it is a fifth below, which is different. It's an F–the inversion of G. It is below the horizon line: moving five steps down the scale. On page 27, Fig. 11, notice the 5 and the 7 o'clock locations; F and G are the inversions of one another and both equidistant from the root.

An interesting fact is inversions always add up to nine. Also, their polarities always change–from major to minor or minor to major. However, perfect remains perfect. Examples: a fifth above = a fourth below when added together = 9; a seventh above = a second below = 9; a sixth above = a third below = 9. More examples include the minor second as the inversion of the major seventh; the minor sixth is the inversion of the major third, etc.

The reason for this phenomenon is the point of intersection of the "scale/letters" and the "circle/numbers." The numbers are all uniform and move away from the center. The vertical letters are on a continuum–moving through the major scale with the same continuing pattern; the ascending scale repeats at the horizon line.

Music is the movement of sound to reach the soul for the education of its virtue".

–Plato (429-347 BCE)

Intervals and Inversions - Examples in Songs

	ASCENDING	DESCENDING
Octave	Somewhere Over the Rainbow	Singin in the Rain
Minor Second	JAWS Till There Was You Joy to the World	Isn't She Lovely O Little Town of Bethlehem
Major Second	Mary Had a Little Lamb Silent Night - Danny Boy	Happy Birthday Three Blind Mice
Minor Third	Brahms Lullaby	Greensleeves Frosty the Snowman Hey Jude
Major Third	Michael Row the Boat Ashore Swing Low Sweet Chariot From the Halls of Montezuma	When The Saints Go Marching In Summertime
Perfect Fourth	Here Comes the Bride I've been Working on the Railroad	Amazing Grace Oh Come All Ye Faithful
Augmented Fourth Flat Fifth	Maria (West Side Story) Purple Haze	
Perfect Fifth	Just the Way You Look Tonight Feelings Twinkle, Twinkle Little Star	Baa Baa Black Sheep It Don't Mean a Thing
Minor Sixth	Love Story The Entertainer	
Major Sixth	Nobody Knows the Trouble I've Seen My Bonnie Lies Over the Ocean	Hush Little Baby Don't Say a Word
Dominant Seventh	Lady Jane Somewhere (West Side Story)	Watermelon Man
Major Seventh	Bali Ha'i (South Pacific)	

Fig. 13. This chart represents intervals and inversions of familiar tunes.

"Music melts all the separate parts of our bodies together."

– Anaïs Nin (1903-1977)

Chromatic Intervals and Inversions - 12 Notes

Fig. 14. Constellation of all chromatic scales - Each slice to is comparable to any other slice, the black circles reveal the chromatic scale for the notes located in that slice for that key. This holds true for each slice. The slice concept enables rotation and the ability to transpose and unlock the same pattern in all the other keys. Scales are bidirectional; they radiate and ascend from the center and descend from the outside circumference ring toward the center.

Compare this graphic with the image on the next page.

Fig. 15. This graphic is flipped on its vertical axis and provides a mirror image for inversions.

Recognize that the slices are relational, inverted by color and by position. Also, the text descriptors are backward, reinforcing the concept of the "opposite," the mirror image—the inversion equidistant from the root and then inverted with a note name. In other words, the distances from the root remain the same. Each slice has a mirror image and opposite positioning, with functions and intervals, except the "Root" and its counterpart, the "b5" or #4. These two notes are in the polar positions, diametrically and halfway across the globe—the highest and lowest points on the globe. The flat fifth is known as a dissonant sound.

Chromatic Scale - 12 Notes

Fig.16. Two ways to realize the chromatic scale. Start with the C near the center of the pie and move vertically; or start at 12 o'clock and rotate clockwise. Each slice and concentric arc represents the next ascending note in order, identified by the small black circle(s) with a white letter/symbol. Start with these twelve notes–pick and choose the desired notes–eliminate the rest. One's choice of numbers, notes and spacings form all the possible chords and scale patterns. In this example, engage the second string (B) on the first fret, as the starting point of C. Move up the fretboard one fret at a time to the thirteenth fret. Use the string (B) first fret, as the starting point of C. Move up the fretboard one fret at a time to the thirteenth fret.

C Major Scale - 7 Notes

Fig. 17. The C major scale pattern is provided in two views: the slice and the circumference. The locations of the SOLID BLACK circles block the accidental notes and subsequently the major scale is formed.

Notice the order, spacing and arrangement of the completely black circles compared to the previous page. This model is used to transpose to all the major scales in all keys. This pattern is the template for both the major scale and the Ionian mode. This pattern works in each slice and in every key. The black circles on the circumference–these notes are not part of the Key of C–just the ones with letters.

Notice the similarity of the location and spacing of black circles to the ebony keys on a piano.

Use this pattern as the template of seven notes found in the chromatic family for all the major scale formulations.

The images on the previous spread compare the chromatic scale to the seven-note major scale. These seven notes are represented by the white text in the slice. The non-accidentals, notes flats (b) and sharps (#) are blocked and not used in the scale.

Move from the center C to the outside and **ASCEND** through the major scale, illustrating the "centrifugal force" concept, moving out and away from the center.

Start at 12 o'clock position and notice the yellow wedge with the eight notes; the C repeats at the top and bottom. This range and scale flow from C to C (C - D - E - F - G - A - B - C). Navigate to the "C" near the center, move up in a straight line, and **ASCEND** the major scale.

From the outside ring at 12 o'clock on the circumference of the circle–start at C, move toward the center and **DESCEND** the major scale C - B - A - G - F - E - D - C. Descending through the major scale demonstrates the "centripetal force" concept "down the drain," or whirlpool effect.

On the circumference, clockwise ascends and counterclockwise descends.

These notes compose the major scale. It is commonly referred to with any of the following terms: the Major Scale, "Do-Re-Mi" or Diatonic Scale. It is also known as the Ionian Mode. The major scale consists of seven notes based on the following spacing and step pattern:

whole-whole-half-whole-whole-whole-half
The eighth degree of this scale is the octave–which repeats.

From this viewpoint, one can see the notes constituting the major scale and their relational orientation to one another. These seven notes starting at the center with C, may be assigned numbers: 1, 2, 3, 4, 5, 6, 7, 8. These numbers correlate to notes and letters. All notes in the C major scale are "non-accidental" notes, meaning no flats or sharps.

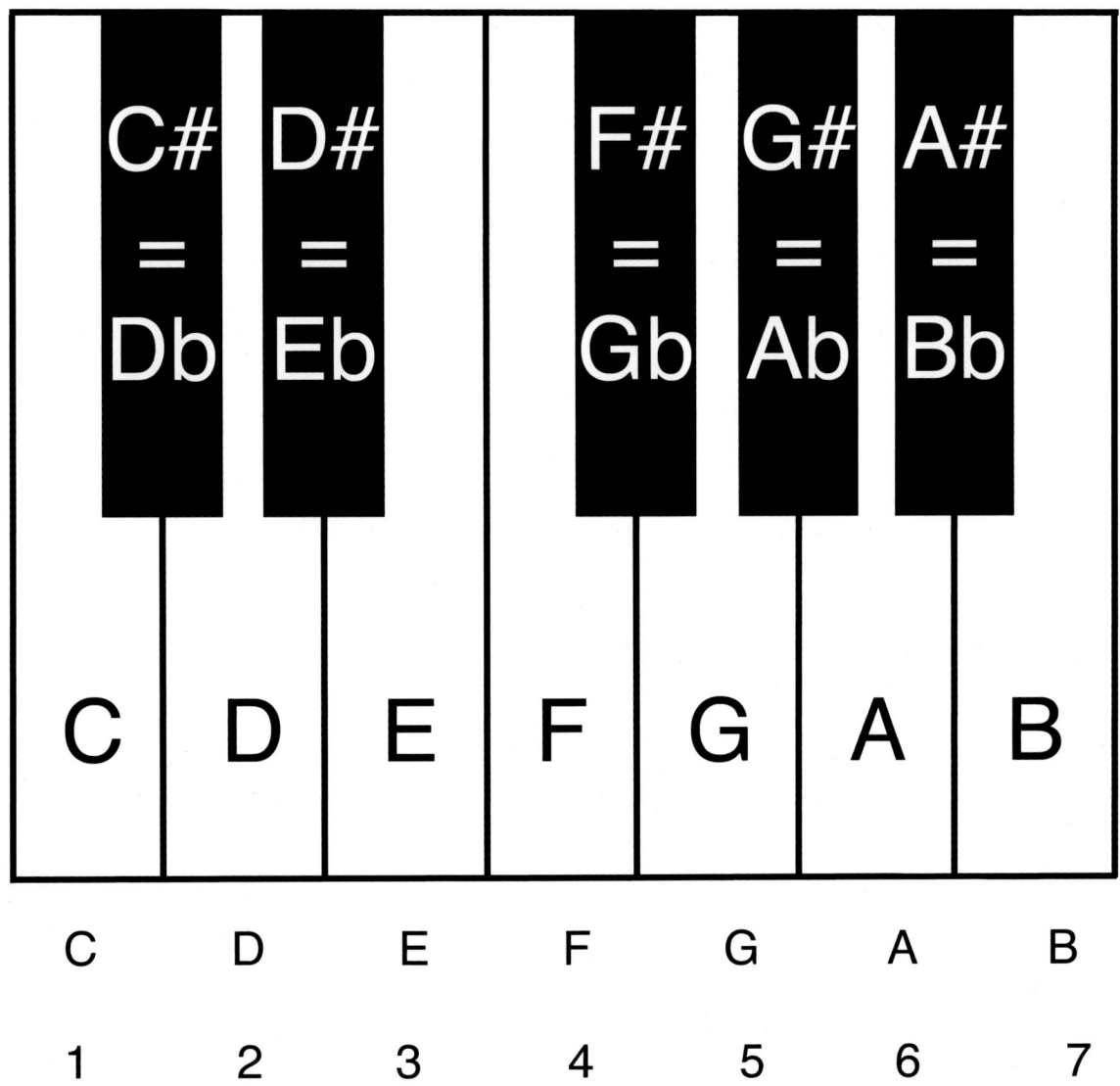

Fig.18. This graphic represents the piano keyboard layout, with the white keys representing the notes of the C major scale. Notice and compare the spatial relationship of the numbers and the letters, especially between B - C and E - F. These seven notes and numbers compose the C Major Scale and the C repeats. This is one register.

"Real understanding does not come from what we learn in books; it comes from what we learn from love of nature, of music, of man. For only what is learned in that way is truly understood."

– Pablo Casals (1876-1973)

Pentatonic Scale - 5 Notes

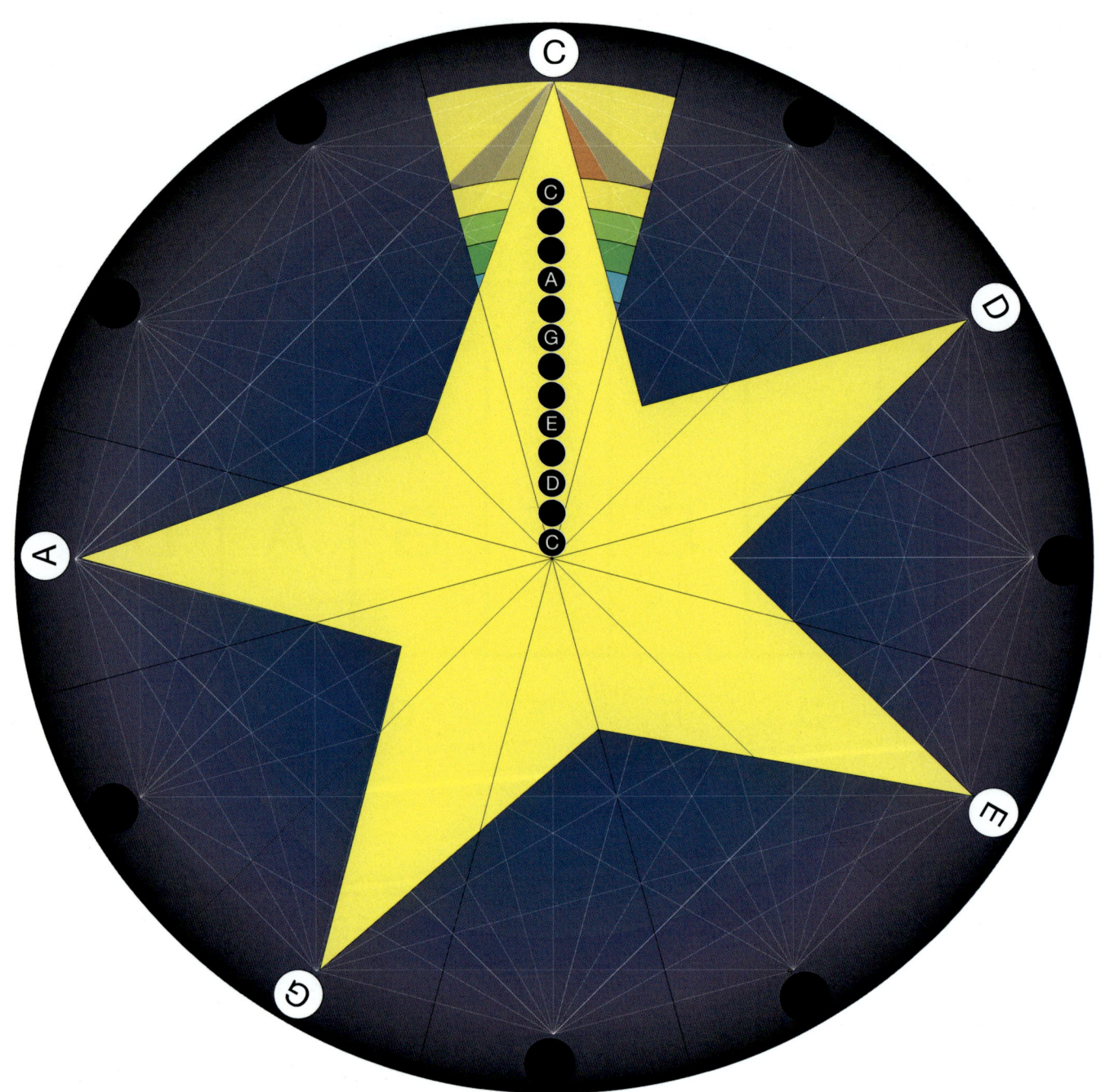

Fig.19. Two ways to realize the pentatonic scale. Start with the C near the center of the pie and move vertically or start at 12 o'clock and rotate clockwise. C - D - E - G -A are the notes of this scale.

Different Names Describe the Same Thing

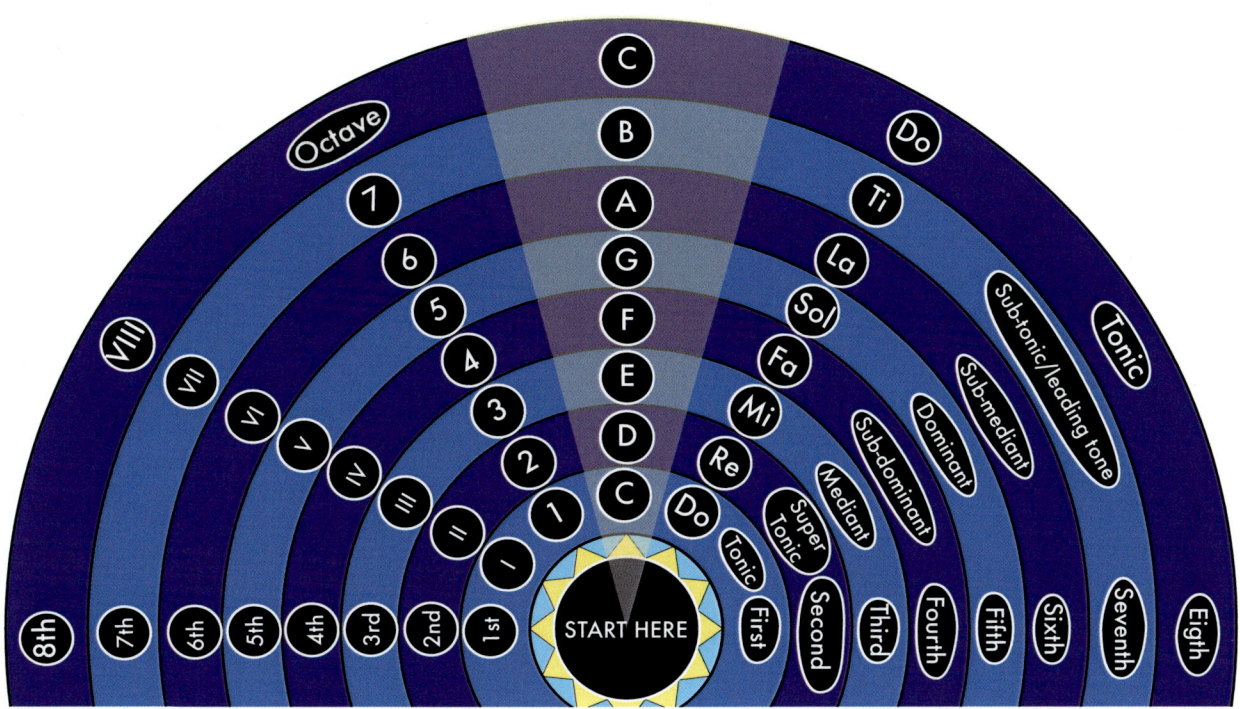

Fig. 20. This image of the C Major Scale is described by equivalent names: C diatonic, the C major, the Do-Re-Mi scale and the C Ionian Mode. Each describes the same choices and spacing arrangements of notes; however, each has a different name–or descriptor.

The graphic above is extrapolated–all items in the same ring express the same function. Start with the row of circles closest to the center on the bottom left. One sees the 1st - Cardinal Numbers, followed by the Roman Numerals, the Ordinal numbers, the Letters, then Do-Re-Mi, and finally the interval names. Each item in the same concentric ring is equivalent in function to the other descriptors in the same ring: the note, the name, the letter, the number, the tonic, etc. Look at the vertical slice and the slice on each side of it: C - D - E (=) 1 - 2 - 3 (=) Do-Re-Mi. Within the same concentric circle, all things are equivalent, substitutable and are different ways of saying the same thing. Each standalone concentric ring is the same and relational in functionality to the rest of the content in that concentric ring; for example: 1st, I, 1, C, Do, Tonic, First. All are equal.

The vertical slice is interchangeable with the major scale of all other of the other keys. All things remain relative and in perfect alignment. Solfège, or solfeggio, is another way to say Do-Re-Mi. The alpha/numeric entities also identify the function descriptor.

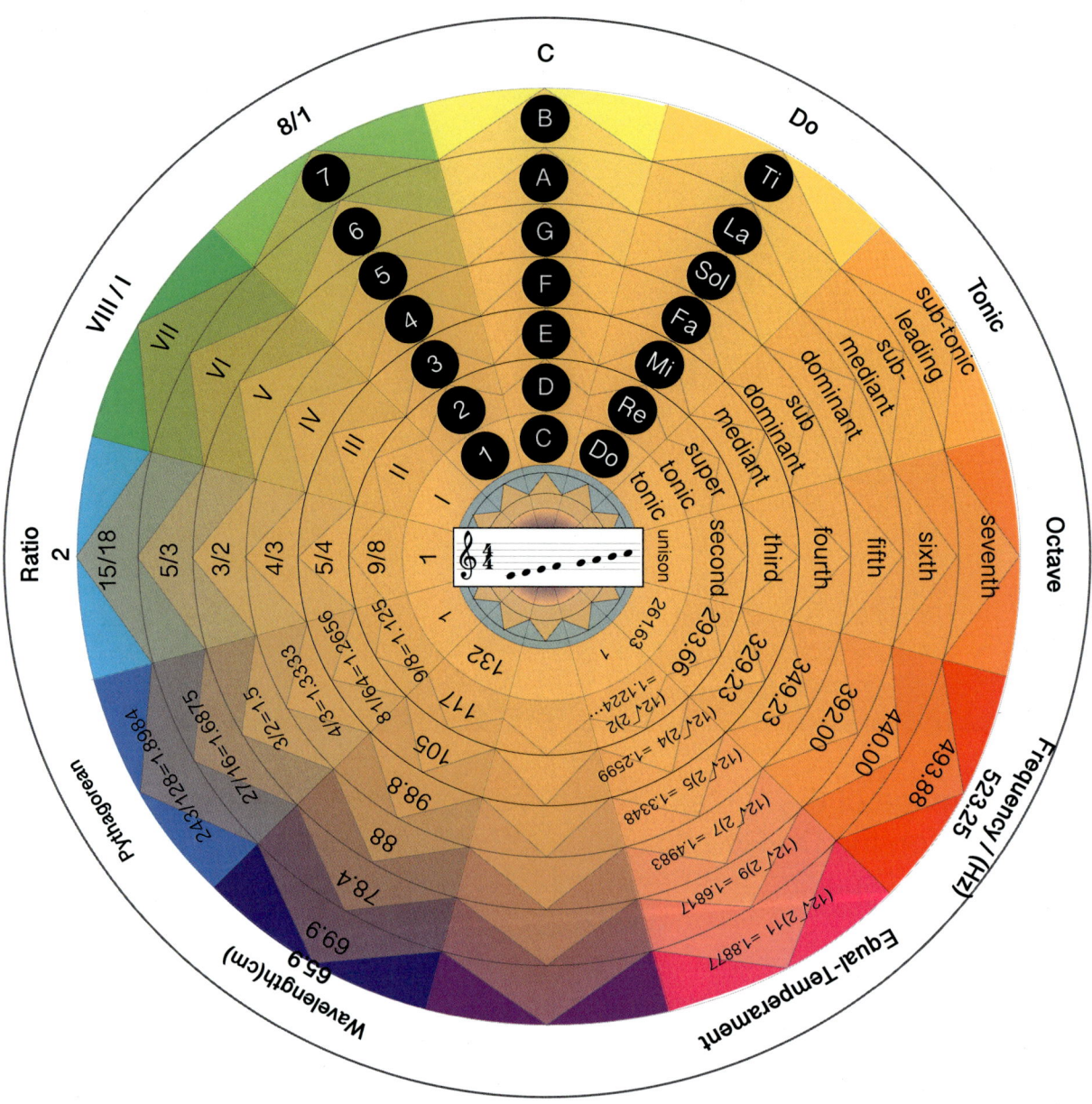

Fig. 21. This diagram of rings expresses relationships using numbers, letters, words, symbols, ratios, wavelengths and frequencies, all are different ways of describing the same thing: 1-2-3 = C-D-E = Do-Re-Mi; all are the same. All contents within the same circle is equivalent to all the other elements in the same concentric circle.

"Color is all. When color is right, form is right. Color is everything, color is vibration like music; everything is vibration."

–Marc Chagall (1903-1977)

Degrees of Scale = Do-Re-Mi Pattern

View the following sequence—one golden arc at a time—representing the motion of the ascending notes in the major scale.

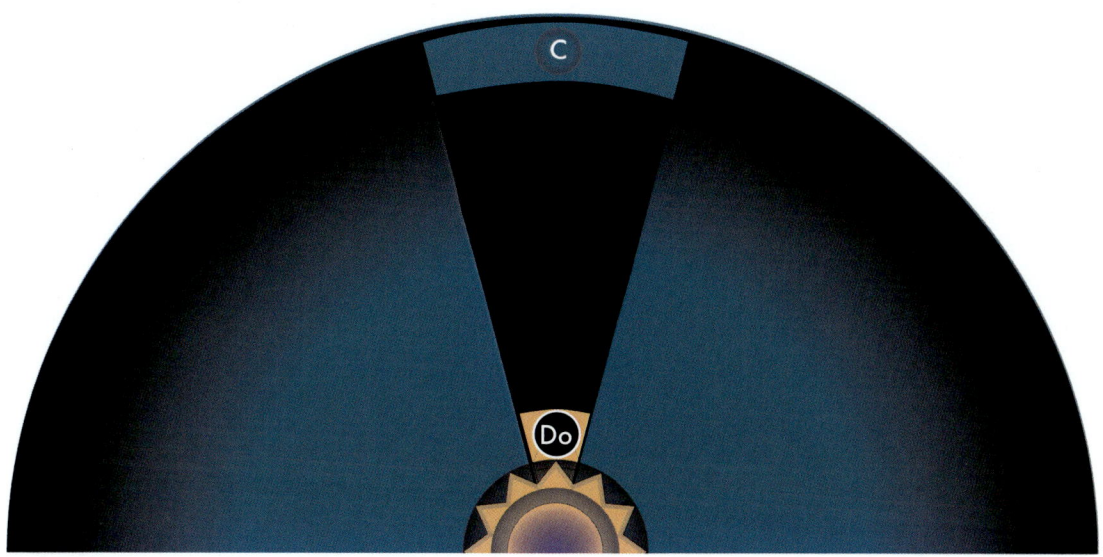

Fig. 22. First Degree. Do = First = One = C

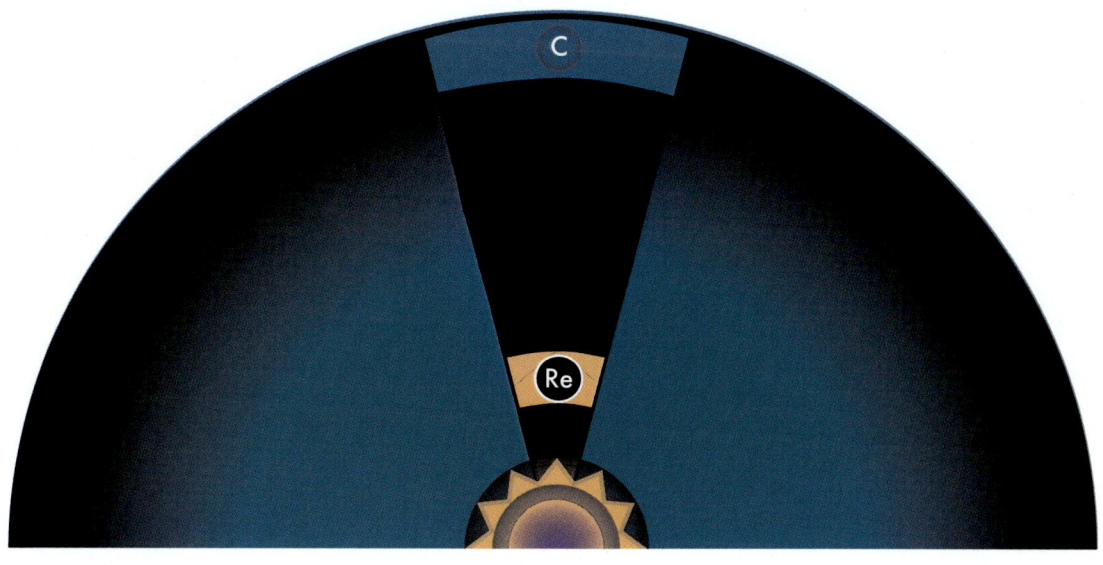

Fig. 23. Second Degree. Re = Second = Two = D

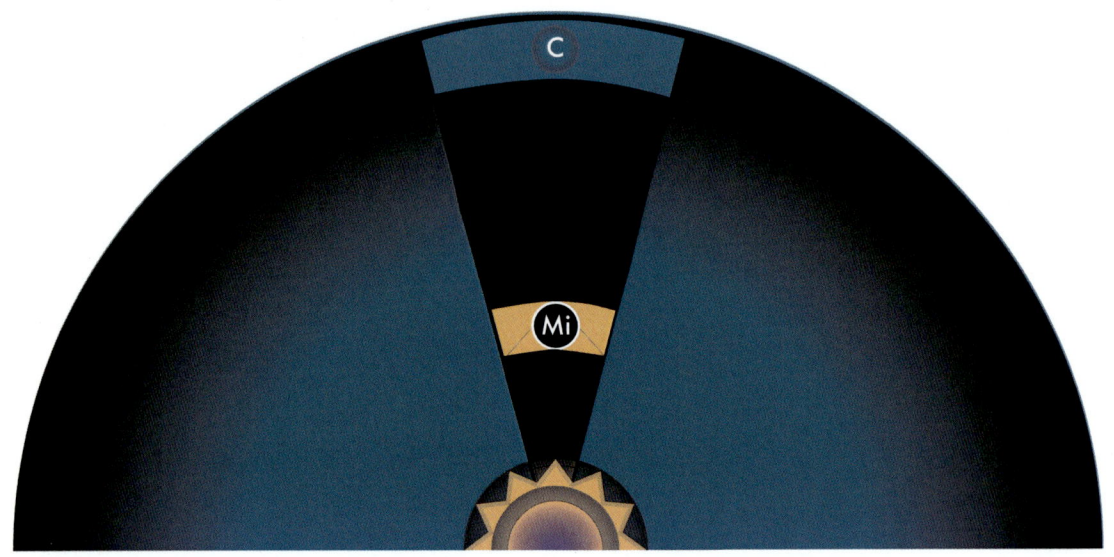

Fig. 24. Third Degree. Mi = Third = Three = E

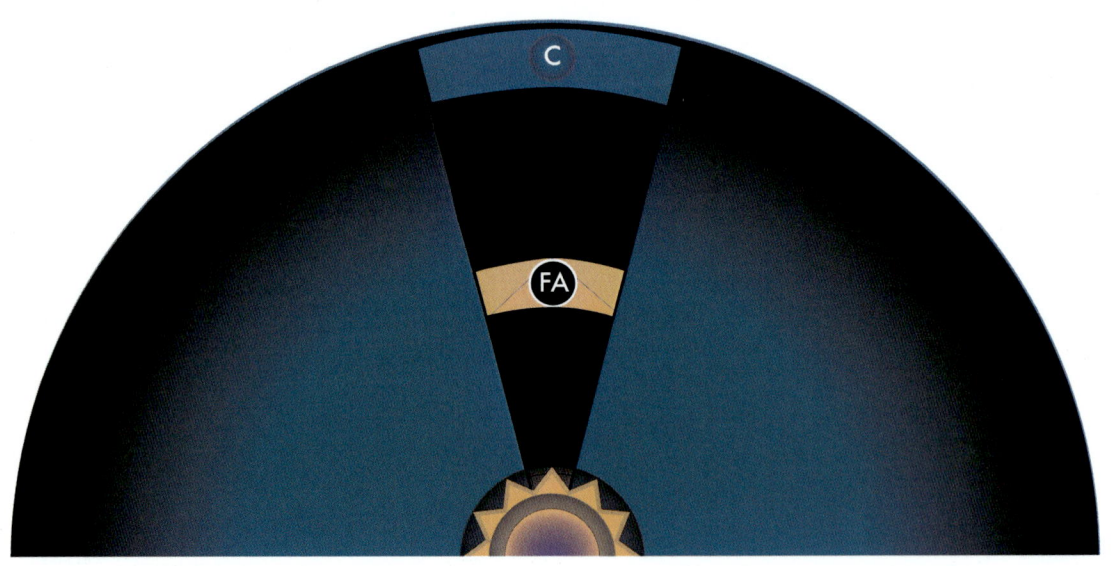

Fig. 25. Fourth Degree. Fa = Fourth = 4 = F

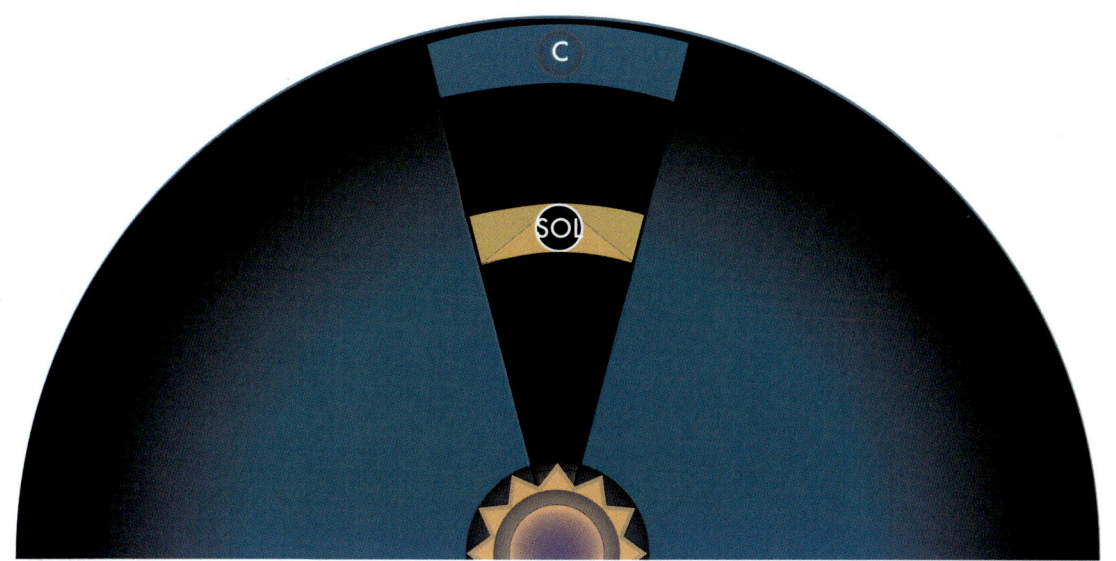

Fig. 26. Fifth Degree. Sol = Fifth = Five = G

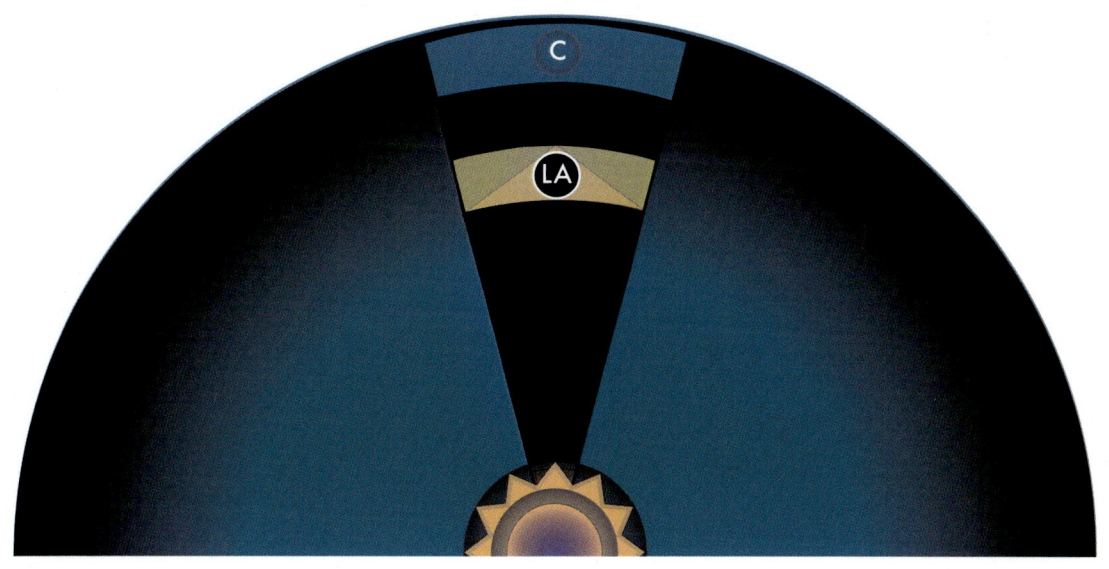

Fig. 27. Sixth Degree. La = Sixth = Six = A

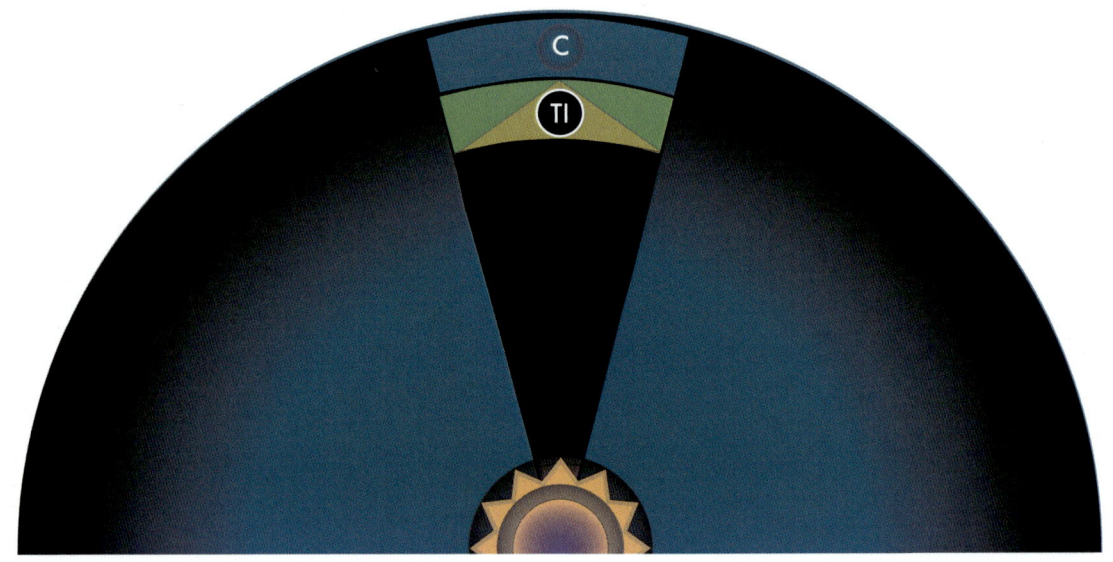

Fig. 28. Seventh Degree. Ti = Seventh = Seven = B

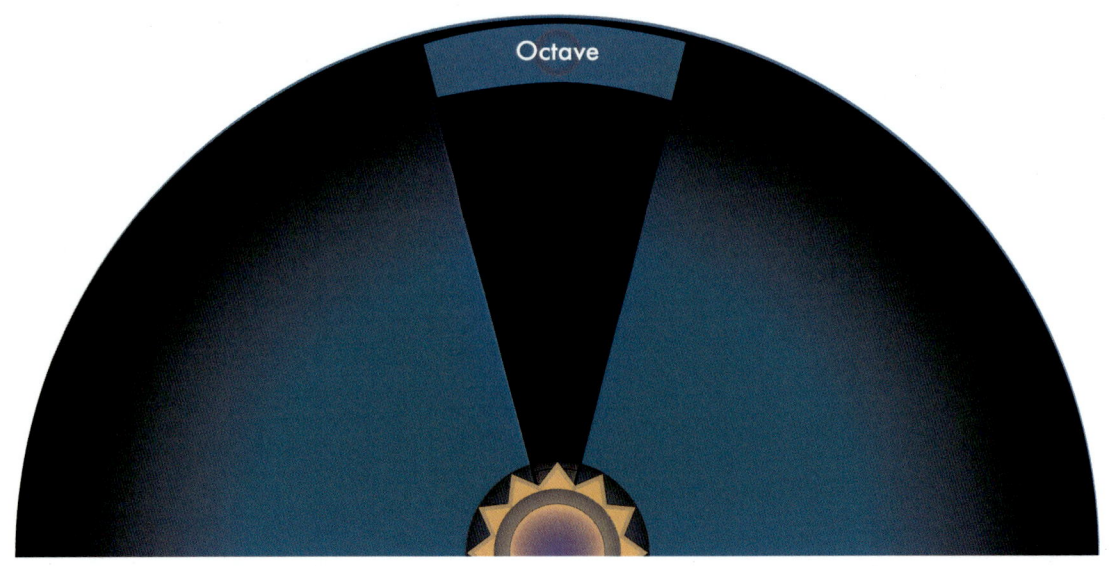

Fig. 29. Eighth Degree. Do = Octave Eight = C = One

~ OCTAVE ~
Back to the Beginning!

Signatures

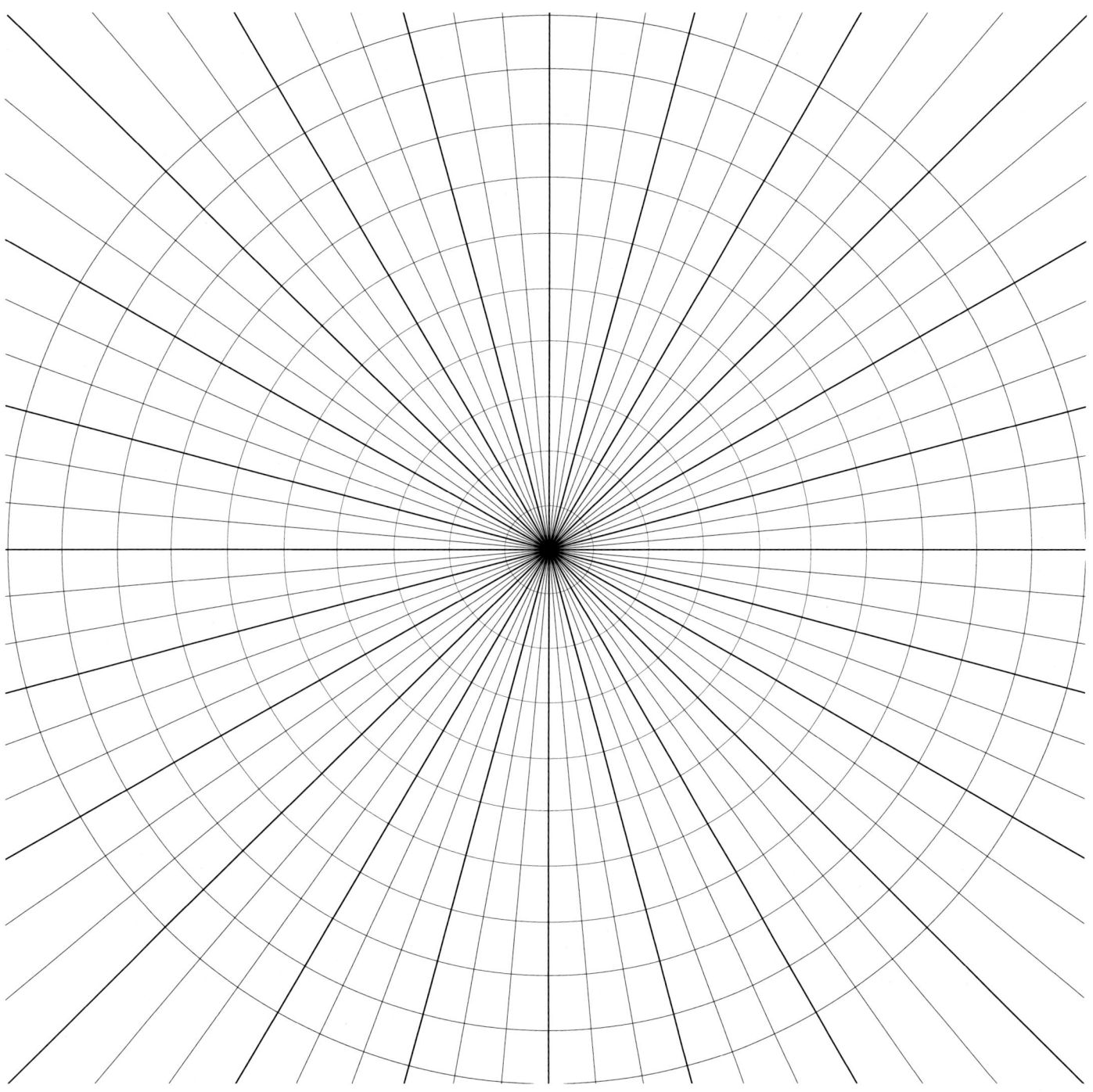

"It gives soul to the universe, wings to the mind, flight to the imagination, and charm and gaiety to life and to everything."

—Plato (429-347 BCE)

Time Signatures

Time Signatures		
Whole note 1 beat for one measure		Whole Note
Half notes 2 beats for one measure		Half Notes
Quarter notes 4 beats for one measure		Quarter Notes
Eighth note 8 beats for one measure		Eighth Notes
Sixteenth note 16 beats for one measure		Sixteenth Notes
Thirty-second note 32 beats for one measure		Thirty-Sec- onds Notes
Rests	Whole Half Eighth Sixteenth Thirty-second Quarter	

Fig. 30. Time signatures. Time signatures are ratios describing the number of beats over a "time duration" known as a "bar" or a "measure."

Common time signatures include: 4/4 (four quarter notes or four beats per measure). 2/4 or "cut time" (two quarter notes per measure or bar (1-2, 1-2) found in marches; 3/4 is often used for waltzes, (three quarter notes per measure or bar (1-2-3, 1-2-3), (5/4, 7/4 are additional time signatures); 6/8 refers to six eighth notes/beats forming a measure found in Jazz, Latin music and a lot of the 1950's Pop.

Time duration is filled with beats and based on fractions. A beat creates the pulse and the feel. Rests and silence are the empty spaces with time allotments. Notice the halving or doubling relationships; one, two, four, eight, sixteen and thirty-two. The whole note has a light spot in the middle. The half-note is light in the center with a "flag pole". The notes are black circles with differing flags. Eighth notes have a connecting flag; the sixteenth notes have two connecting flags. Each increment decreases and manipulates the time duration. Three flags represent the 32rh note. Observe the rests and their variations. The rest start with small rectangles affixed above and below a staff line. There are additional glyphs representing other times for rest.

Music Staff and Tablature

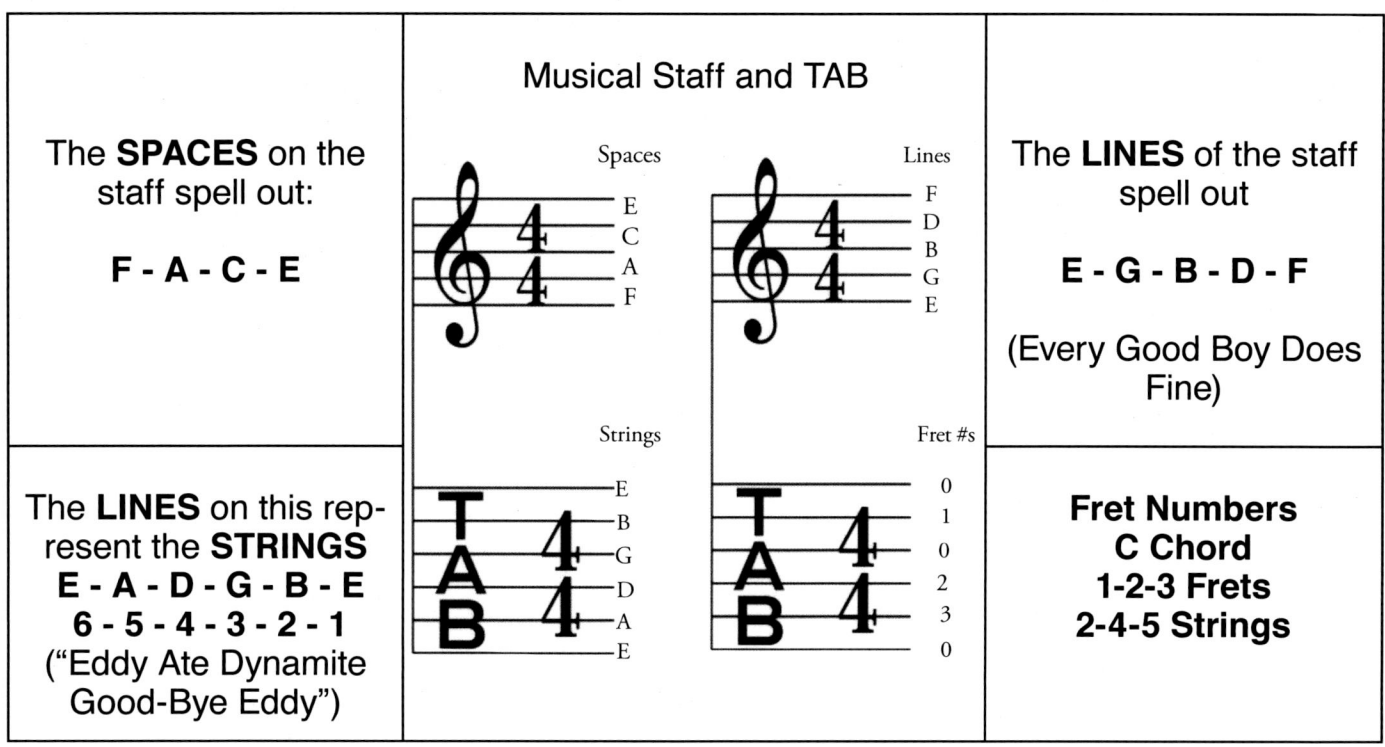

	Musical Staff and TAB	
The **SPACES** on the staff spell out: **F - A - C - E**	Spaces: E C A F	The **LINES** of the staff spell out **E - G - B - D - F** (Every Good Boy Does Fine)
	Lines: F D B G E	
The **LINES** on this represent the **STRINGS** **E - A - D - G - B - E** **6 - 5 - 4 - 3 - 2 - 1** ("Eddy Ate Dynamite Good-Bye Eddy")	Strings: E B G D A E	**Fret Numbers** **C Chord** **1-2-3 Frets** **2-4-5 Strings**
	Fret #s: 0 1 0 2 3 0	

Fig. 31. This chart is divided into separate entities. The top represents the Staff, the conventional way of presenting and transcribing music. The upper left represent the SPACES, which spells FACE. The upper right depicts the lines on the staff, and are represented by the letter E, G, B, D, F; a simple way to remember this is: **E**very **G**ood **B**oy **D**oes **F**ine.

The lower portion represents the Tablature, a contemporary way to show music for the guitarists, known as TAB. On the lower left side, the horizontal lines represent the strings of the guitar with the bass on the bottom. The lower right side represents the fret numbers on each string. This gives you the location and string for each of your desired notes.

"If I were not a physicist, I would probably be a musician. I often think in music. I live my daydreams in music. I see my life in terms of music."

–Albert Einstein (1879-1955)

Key Signatures

Flat Keys		Accidentals	Sharp Keys	
Signature	Major and Relative Minor share the same Key signature	0	Major and Relative Minor share the same Key signature	Signature
	—	C A Minor 0	—	
	F D Minor	1	G E Minor	
	Bb G Minor	2	D B Minor	
	Eb C Minor	3	A F# Minor	
	Ab F Minor	4	E C# Minor	
	Db Bb Minor	5	B G# Minor	
	Gb Eb Minor	6	F# D# Minor	
	Cb Ab Minor	7	C# A# Minor	

Fig. 32. The key signatures are located at the beginning of a composition. This information is presented with the flat signatures on the left and the sharp signatures are on the right. The flats increase by fourths and the sharps increase by fifths. This arrangement on the left is the order of sub dominants, the right is order of dominants.

Signatures are unique. Each is identified with the appropriate location and number of sharps or flats. These two factors identify the key, i.e., which notes are flatted or sharped. Notice that the yellow rectangle; this represents the Key of C. The Signature has NO flats and NO sharps. Another important aspect to see in this graphic is the Major and Relative Minor relationships, these two share the same Key Signature, and the range is able to be substituted.

Relative Minors

Each key signature represents both the major key and its relative minor scale. The yellow rectangle represents the key of C, with no flats or sharps, as shown in the key signature. The relative minor is the "A minor," which starts on the sixth note of the C major scale. It shares the same notes as the C major scale–the only difference is its starting point: the six note as opposed to the one note. The similarity is the fact that–both use the same notes and spacings–just starting at a different origin point, either the C (1) or A (6). The sixth degree of a major scale is the relative minor, it is often substituted for the one chord.

The columns on the previous page are organized into a particular order: on the left side–notice the additive sequence identifying all the flat keys. On the right side, notice the additive sequence used for the identification of all the sharp keys.

On the next page, find Fig. 32, see the numbers of flats and sharps increase incrementally from C in both directions with each slice. One flat represents the key of F (one slice to the left of the C vertical slice–11 o'clock); two flats represent the key of Bb (two to the left of the C vertical slice–10 o'clock) and so on moving counterclockwise on the outside ring of the diagram. Rotating clockwise reveals the sharp keys (one to the right and continuing clockwise); each incremental step adds one more sharp to the key signature. G has one sharp, D has two sharps, A has three sharps, etc. The sequence represents the circle of fifths and order of dominants. With this different arrangement, start at the 12 and move in a clockwise direction along the outside scale. Each slice is a fifth above. Move in a counterclockwise rotation and each slide is a fourth degree above. Pick any "center slice" along the circumference. One slice to the right is always a fifth, and one to the left is always a fourth. This is an important concept for developing progressions for songs and tunes.

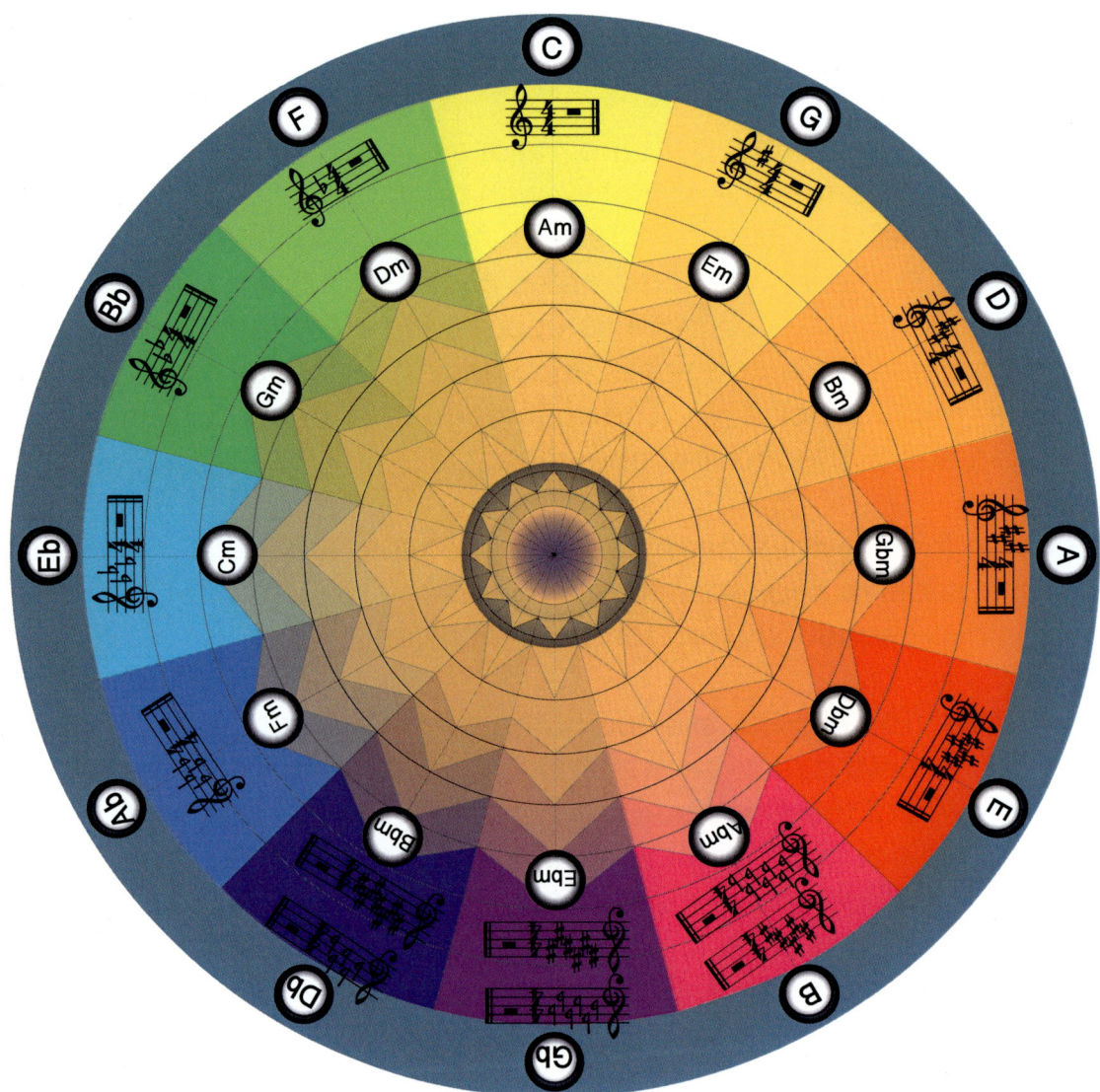

Fig. 33. The high-lighted circles in white on the circumference represent the key, The interior white circles–inside the slice–represent the sixth degree and the relative minor. (Example: C to Am).

The other 11 slices are equivalent except each is a different key. The outside circle is the key; the rectangular glyphs are the Key and Time Signatures. The circle inside indicates the relative minor–the sixth degree of the scale.

At the bottom there are three overlapping keys. Each has two signatures–identifying key signatures that employ both flat(s) or sharp(s). These are known as "Enharmonic Equivalents" and can be described by both groups–either sharped or flatted.

Numbers and Math

Numbers and math play a significant role in music and theory. There are basic sequences found in music that are also mirrored and measured in math. These underlying measurements are valuable places to begin, understand, know and use in writing songs and developing compositions.

Its a matter of scale. One through five, one through seven and one through twelve are three of the primary numeric sequences found in musical scales. In order of simplicity, these three groupings represent: (1.) The pentatonic (five note, major/minor) scale, (2.) Diatonic (seven note, major/minor) scale, and (3.) the chromatic scale.

Use the first three odd numbers of the major scale: 1 - 3 - 5. This outlines the major chord structure (basic triad), while the even numbers 2 - 4 - 6 equate to a minor chord structure; and it shares a close relationship to the sub-dominant F chord (four = 4). Notice the D minor is the relative minor of F.

Each grouping of notes offers different, unique patterns, creative options for expressing music. Each pattern is unique to itself and relational to its key. There is a virtually unlimited universe of music from which to build, create and express emotions. By choosing and embellishing chords in the sequence of the major scale, a harmonized scale is realized.

When visualizing the whole picture of music and its many inter relational aspects, it would be incomplete without recognizing there is so much more than just sequential numbers. These result in odd/even patterns. It is vital to look deeper into the values, ranges, scales, and all that makes the music constellation "infinite."

By describing music with numbers, one is able to observe certain "constant" relationships; for instance, the "basic triad" chord is the: 1 - 3 - 5 degrees/notes of the major scale. Perhaps the most well-known is the basic progression composed of chords based on the 1 - 4 - 5 degrees of the major scale. These are simple ways to identify the chord progression and the value (i.e., the functions = tonic, sub-dominant, dominant). All equal numbers are equal in function for example, in all keys: sixths are relative to the one note. These are able to be substituted for the Root or the One chord). All chords that are a fifth are considered to be dominant, often accompanied with a dominant seventh note.

Looking deeper into the numeric functions, one finds proven and known ratios and proportions that identify measurement attributes. From the math experience, one knows the formula for finding the area(s) and circumference(s) of circles uses pi. The factor of pi equals 3.14..... In addition to pi, there are formulas for identifying universal ratios and patterns found throughout music, as well as nature, regardless of scale.

Phi is a ratio: 1.614—and it defines qualities in art and design attributes. Within art, architectural and design, patterns conform to this "relational formula," including the pyramids and the Parthenon in ancient Greece. There is a direct relationship of harmonic frequencies and natural signatures within the visible spectrum and the realm of physics. Within nature, one finds "golden proportions" that are pleasing to the eye and provide a sense of harmony, natural beauty and design. Some examples of phi are evidenced and arranged in nature; examples are identified by the spirals found on outsides of pine cones and pineapples. Another example is the seed placement found in sunflowers. This is true for music composition and artistic design, as well.

Sacred geometry historically has permeated our world. Universally speaking, all things are divine and aligned. The Fibonacci sequence of numbers is based on a pattern starting with zero and adding the previous two integers. This sequence is as follows: 0, 1, 1, 2, 3, 5, 8, 13, 21, etc. This pattern can be used for choices of note options, as well as, the relational aspects to temporal and spatial locations in compositions. Examples of these patterns have been used by Mozart, Satie and many other composers, Expressionists and improvisers.

Notice the first numbers in this Fibonacci sequence: 0 - 1 - 3 - 5 - 8 - 13. These numbers are building blocks and the foundation in music: 1 - 3 - 5 - 8 - 13. The 1 - 3 - 5 is the basic triad of primary chords. The 8th is the octave. The 13th is the highest extreme, or a start identifying a new register or range.

"Your body is the harp of your soul and it is yours to bring forth sweet music from it or confused sounds."

–Kahlil Gibran (1883-1931)

Numbers in Rhythm

Use numbers to start and count off songs. Counting helps one to stay on the beat and to know where rhythm patterns fit. Counting helps promote accuracy and precision—on beat—prepared for the next chord changes.

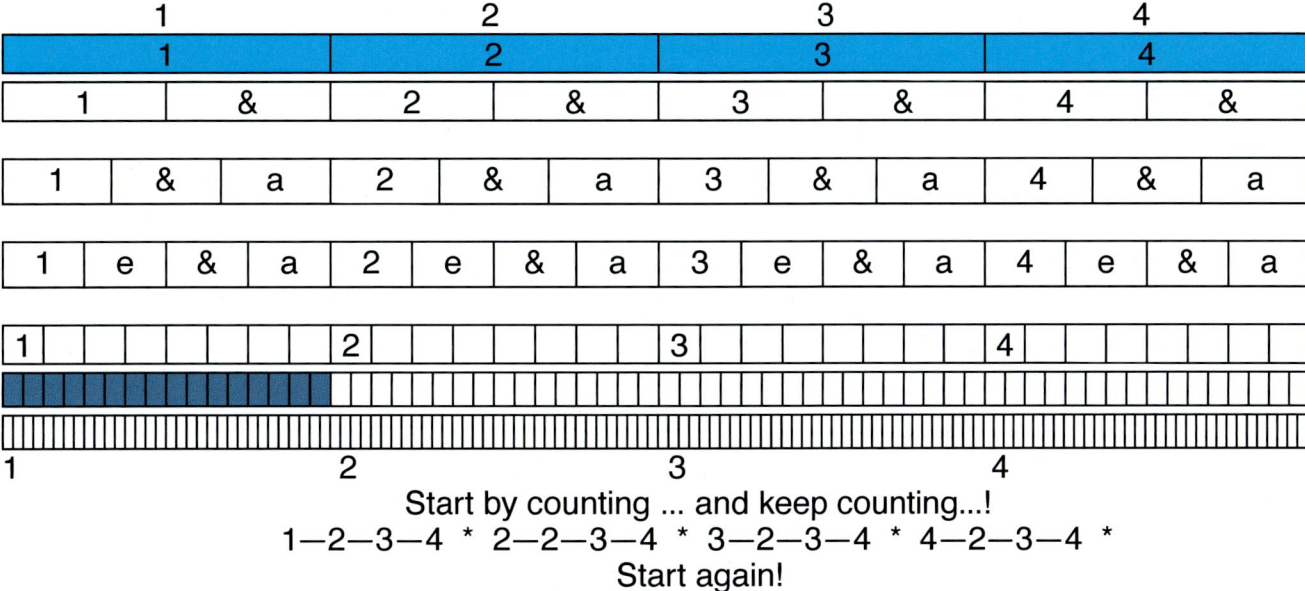

Start by counting ... and keep counting...!
1—2—3—4 * 2—2—3—4 * 3—2—3—4 * 4—2—3—4 *
Start again!

Fig. 35. In the graphic, each line divides the same space into different groupings of time used for rhythmic patterns.

One, Two, Three, Four can also be: **One and, Two and, Three and, Four and.**
One and a, Two and a, Three and a, Four and a. In addition, it can be further divided into **One "e" and "a," two "e" and "a," three "e" and "a," four "e" and "a."**

Numbers in the Chromatic Scale

1	2	3	4	5	6	7	8	9	10	11	12	13	Degrees (°) Numbers (#)
C	C# Db	D	D# Eb	E	F	F# Gb	G	G# Ab	A	A# Bb	B	Octave C	Note Name

Fig. 36. This graphic represents the numbers and their correlating notes and degrees, found in the chromatic scale. The one and the thirteen are the starting points on the scale. In this illustration, the thirteen is a "repeat" and the octave, a new beginning. It starts a new scale in the next higher register.

One can choose other scale patterns to superimpose over the chromatic scale. The choice, order, number and the spacing patterns of the notes form the scales, modes, arpeggios and chords. In addition to the seven note major scale pattern, there are "derivative" patterns, including the minor scales, the pentatonic (five-tone), whole tone (six-tone), augmented and diminished scale forms.

The chromatic scale can start on any note and uses "all" twelve notes in sequential order. Each note is equally spaced–described and measured as a "semi-tone," or a "half-step." This can be viewed in a linear manner with the same recurring note pattern.

The World is Sound

"At the root of all power and motion, there is music and rhythm, the play of patterned frequencies against the matrix of time. We know that every particle in the physical universe takes its characteristics from the pitch and pattern and overtones of its particular frequencies, its singing. Before we make music, music makes us."

–Joachim-Ernst Berendt (1922-2000)

Ascending

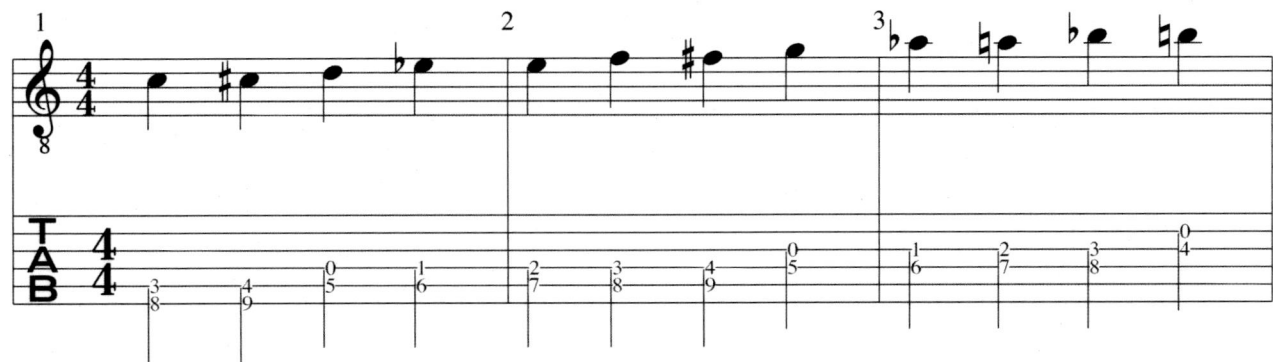

Descending

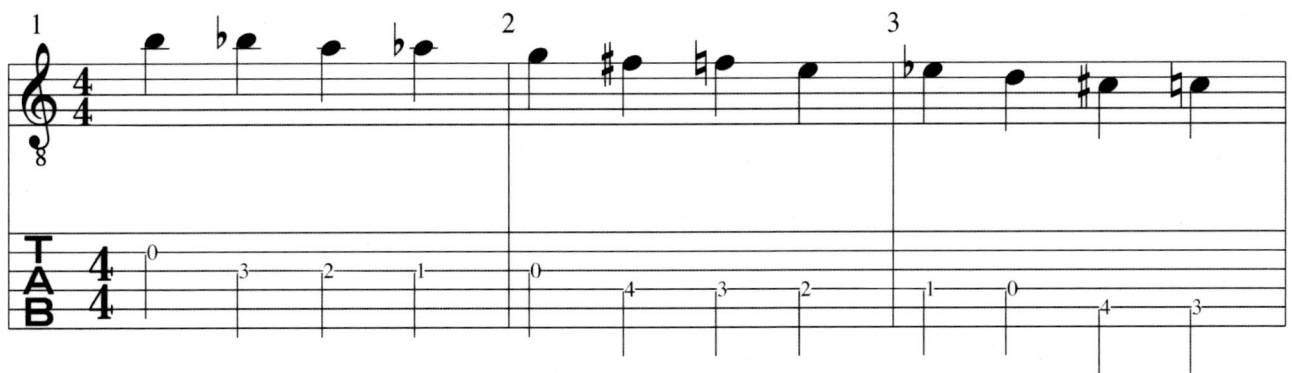

Fig. 37. These two graphic images represent the chromatic scale, each with two sets of lines: one being the traditional staff (5 lines and 4 spaces) and the TAB (tablature) approach for the guitar (strings and frets). Both sets of images represent the same scale and notes. These two groups represent the ascending and the descending sequence of the chromatic scale in C. Each group of lines represent two ways of describing the same thing. In each graphic, the upper portion of the image is the conventional and the traditional way, the lower is the TAB–a way to correlate the string and the fret number for guitar players.

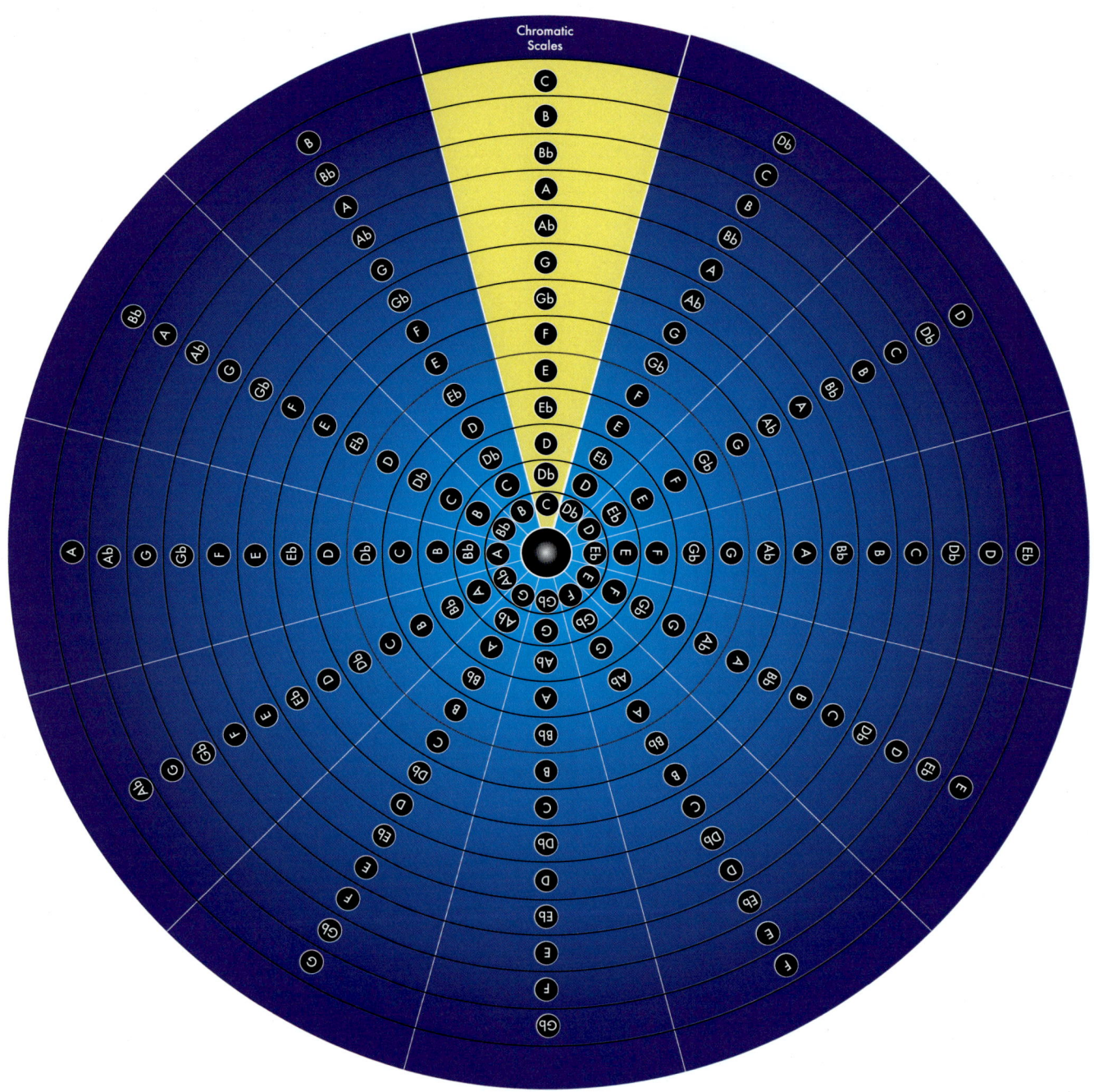

Fig. 38. The above image is a constellation of all the chromatic scales. Scales are bidirectional; they radiate and ascend from the center and descend from the outside circumference ring toward the center The notes of the C chromatic scale are represented in the golden slice.

The preceding three sets of illustrations combined provide three different ways of describing the same thing: notation staff, tablature and the graphic/visual approach. Each slice is a chromatic scale. Remember each concentric circle is a chromatic scale, as well.

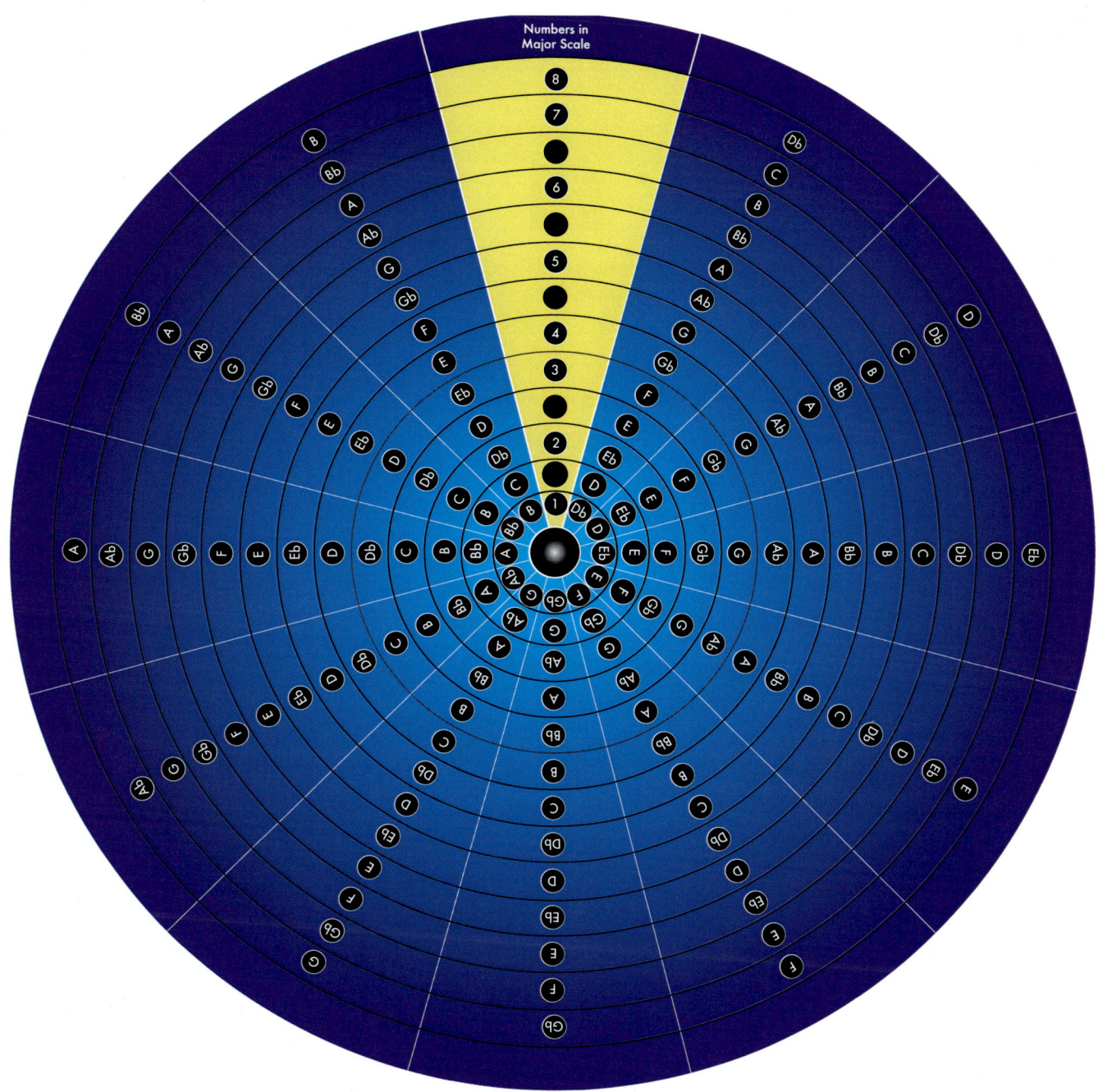

Fig. 39. This image represents the numbers found in the major scale in the key of C (1-7 and the 8 is a repeats of the 1). The major scale is composed of seven notes which correspond to the letters of the scale: C - D - E - F - G - A - B - C.

Compare the image on the previous page representing the whole chromatic scale with this seven-note major scale identified by the white circles. These white dots represent notes of the major scale only. These are the non accidental notes, no flats (b) and no sharps (#). The black dots block the accidental notes in the golden slice.

Numbers in Scales

1	2	3	4	5	6	7	8	9	10	11	12	13	(°s) Degrees
C	C# Db	D	D# Eb	E	F	F# Gb	G	G# Ab	A	A# Bb	B	C	Chromatic
C		D		E	F		G		A		B	C	Major Scale Notes
C		D		E	F		G		A		B	C	Major Scale Letters
1		2		3	4		5		6		7	8	Major Scale Numbers
1				3			5				7		Major 7 Chord

Fig. 40. Scales are relational to one another and to the chromatic scale.

In this example, the "diatonic", major scale is extracted from the chromatic scale notes. One can see the pattern of conversion—a reduction from twelve to seven, resulting in empty spaces, which represent the placeholders from the unused sharps and/or flats. The chromatic line (above) is the same configuration and pattern of the piano keyboard layout of the black and white keys.

The two lines below the green dividing bar (blue and yellow) represent the notes of the C major scale, i.e., letters and numbers. These correspond with the white circles in the previous-page illustration. Recognize the ratio of the seven-to-twelve note pattern and how the spaces correspond to each other.

In the above table, the empty white rectangles on each line represent the non-engaged spaces, the placeholders for keeping the pattern accurate and intact. The dark blue rectangles represent the seven notes in the scale; the white spaces represent the difference from the chromatic. On the previous page, in Fig. 39, the yellow slice represents the numbers of the C scale. Notice and compare the top line (light blue) and the major scale numbers (in yellow). See how their respective numbers are different from the chromatic and seemingly do not correlate. This is a result of being extracted from a different Numeric Base, making the differing ranges, spaces and numbers in the scale—specifically 12 reduced to 7 notes.

The bottom line, labeled "Major 7 Chord," reveals the three notes needed for the basic triad (1 - 3 - 5) plus the major seventh added, to form the major seventh chord.

Numbers in Scales - Major

Major Scale								
C	D	E	F	G	A	B	C	Letter
O		O		O		O		Odd-Dominant Major
	N		N		N		N	Even-Sub-Dom. Minor
1	2	3	4	5	6	7	8	Degree

Fig. 41. There are seven notes, points or degrees composing the major scale. The major scale follows a spacing pattern with a specific ordering pattern of notes. Notice the odd/even aspects.

The spacing of the major scale determines the following sequential arrangement:

Whole Step + Whole Step + Half Step + Whole Step + Whole Step + Whole Step + Half Step

These notes and the spacing order are the template of the major scale. Chords are built from these notes and degrees of the scale. In this example, odd and even numbers occur in the major scale. This fluctuating binary pattern of either "odd or even" "up and down" provides a sine wave, an alternating and oscillating pattern (see diagram below).

---

1 - 3 - 5 - 7 - The odd numbers, under eight, form the major seventh chord.

2 - 4 - 6 - 8 - The even numbers, including eight, form a minor = the second degree with added 7th

| 1 - 3 - 5 - 7 - Odd | 1 = Tonic | 3 = Mediant | 5 = Dominant | 7 = Sub-Tonic |

Wave Pattern

| 2 - 4 - 6 - 8 - Even | 2 = Super Tonic | 4 = Sub-Dom | 6 = Sub-Mediant | 8 = Tonic |

Fig. 42. The odd numbers are the primary numbers found in the major chord. Even numbers form minors the sub dominant type chords–the two chord–is a minor, the four is the sub dominant with the major seventh note. These formations often equate the sounds and functions that are similar to a minor. The fifth is the dominant and major. The sixth is the relative minor and substitutable with the one–or tonic key. And, finally, the seventh is the minor with a "flatted fifth" added and used for harmonic purity. This is known as the "Leading Tone" and "Diminished Triad" (flatted third and flatted fifth).

In the example below, the major scale is called out in letters and numbers:

1 is C, tonic, major scale, first note of the Ionian Mode.
2 is D, the super tonic, minor scale, the first note of the Dorian Mode.
3 is E, the mediant, "secondary relative minor" the first note - Phrygian Mode.
4 is F, the sub dominant, the first note of the Lydian Mode.
5 is G, the dominant, the first note of the Mixolydian Mode.
6 is A, the "relative minor," the first note of the Aeolian Mode.
7 is B, leading tone, B minor7 b5 "diminished" and first note - Locrian Mode.

To create the modes, start with any number and cycle through the whole sequence in order.

Major Scale								
C	D	E	F	G	A	B	C	Alpha
1	2	3	4	5	6	7	8	Numeric

Fig. 43. These same notes, the odd numbers, constitute arpeggios and chords = 1 - 3 - 5 - 7, composed of only the odd numbers. They are the outline, the form, the framework of a chord. Arpeggios are basic triads and extensions played sequentially, up and down.

The numbers of the Major Scale, 1 - 7, provide most of the notes needed for the formation chords. There are four primary triads. These are the: Major, Minor, Augmented and Diminished. These all are a triads, based on three notes: the 1 - 3 - 5 or some variation.

To create the major triad: use the 1 - 3 - 5 degrees of the major scale.
To create the minor triad chord use the 1 - b3 - 5: lower the third (3rd) a half-step.
For the Diminished triad: lower the third (3rd) a half-step, the fifth (5th) a half-step.
For the Augmented triad: keep the major third (3rd), sharp the fifth (5th) a half-step.
To form the seventh chord add the desired seventh degree - major or dominant.
To form the extended chords, use the basic triad, add the major seventh, ninth, eleventh and thirteenth degree.

Numbers - Composing the Basic Triad

Combine the (1 - 3 - 5) notes of the major scale to form the Basic Triad. By adding the seventh degree (+7), the major seventh chord is created. There are two types of sevenths: major 7th and dominant 7th. The difference is a half-step.

Arrive at the **Major 7** by lowering the octave note (down) one **half-step**.

Arrive at a **Dominant 7** by lowering the octave note (down) a **whole step** .

1 - 3 - 5 = Odd numbers - Major
1 - 3 - 5 - 7 = Odd numbers - Major Seventh
1 - 3 - 5 - b7 = Odd numbers - Dominant Seventh

These odd numbers, or degrees, are referred to with the following terms:

1 = Tonic
3 = Mediant
5 = Dominant
7 = Leading Tone/Sub tonic

2 - 4 - 6 - 8 = Even Numbers - Minor / Sub dominant

2 = Super Tonic
4 = Sub dominant
6 = Sub mediant
8 = Octave

The following graphics represent the four types of triads: Major, Minor, Augmented and Diminished. Each graphic has a black heptagon, which represents the C major scale of component notes and the distance (intervals) between each note. The red triangle, or polygon, in each graphic outlines the notes and points of each chord. The fretboard patterns below offer the two fingerings–simple and advanced. Notice the 1 - 3 - 5 are represented in the primary colors: yellow, red and blue.

C Major and C Minor Triad Shapes
Basic Triad 1 - 3 - 5 and Minor Triad 1 - b3 - 5

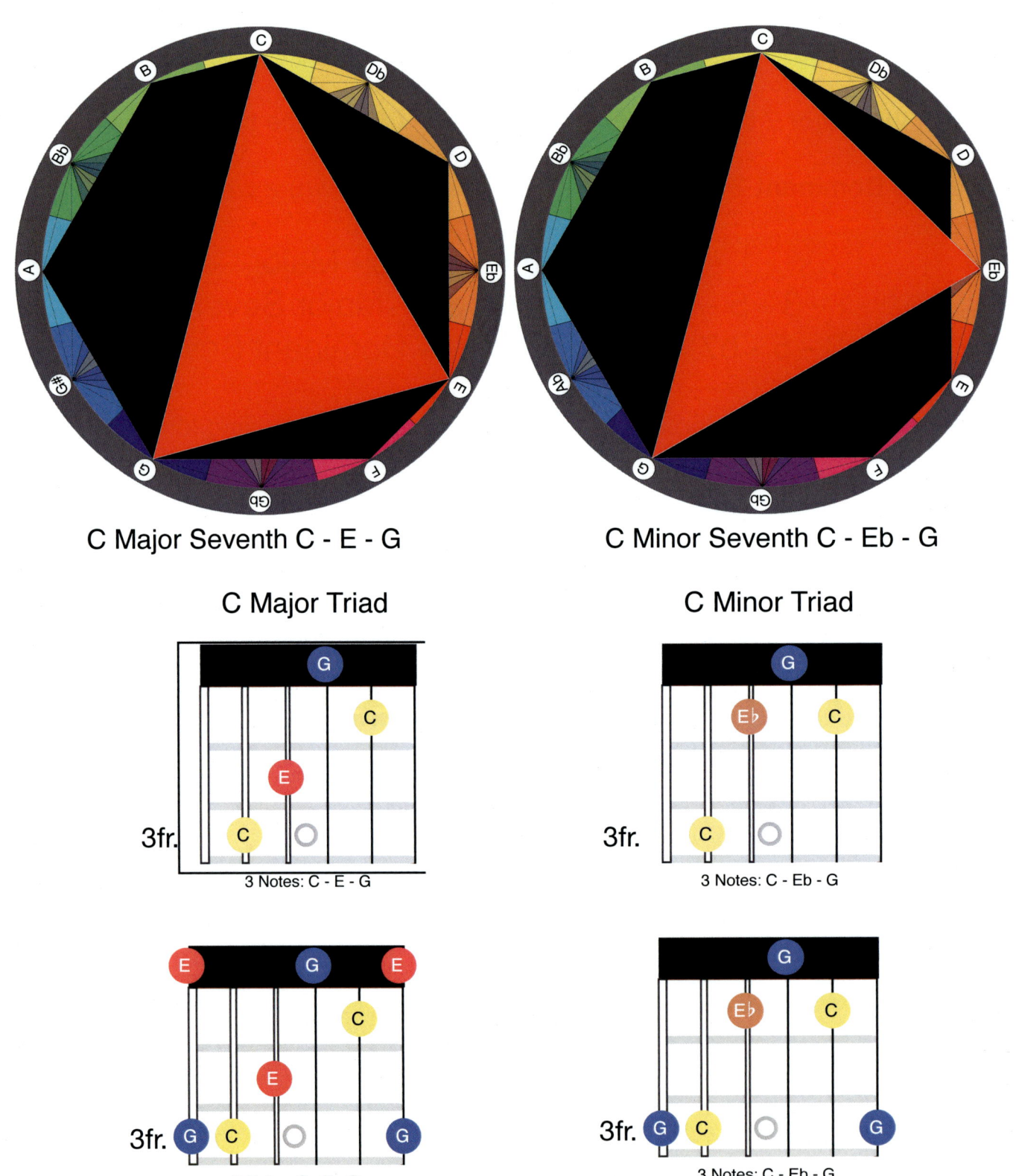

C Major Seventh C - E - G   C Minor Seventh C - Eb - G

C Major Triad   **C Minor Triad**

3fr.   3 Notes: C - E - G   3fr.   3 Notes: C - Eb - G

3fr.   3 Notes: C - E - G   3fr.   3 Notes: C - Eb - G

Fig. 44. The major chord is composed of the 1-3-5. The minor is created by flatting the third (b3) of the major chord. Bottom row is a more advanced view of the C chords.

C Major Seventh and Minor Seventh Shapes
Major 7th: 1 - 3 - 5 - 7 and Minor 7th 1 - b3 - 5 - b7

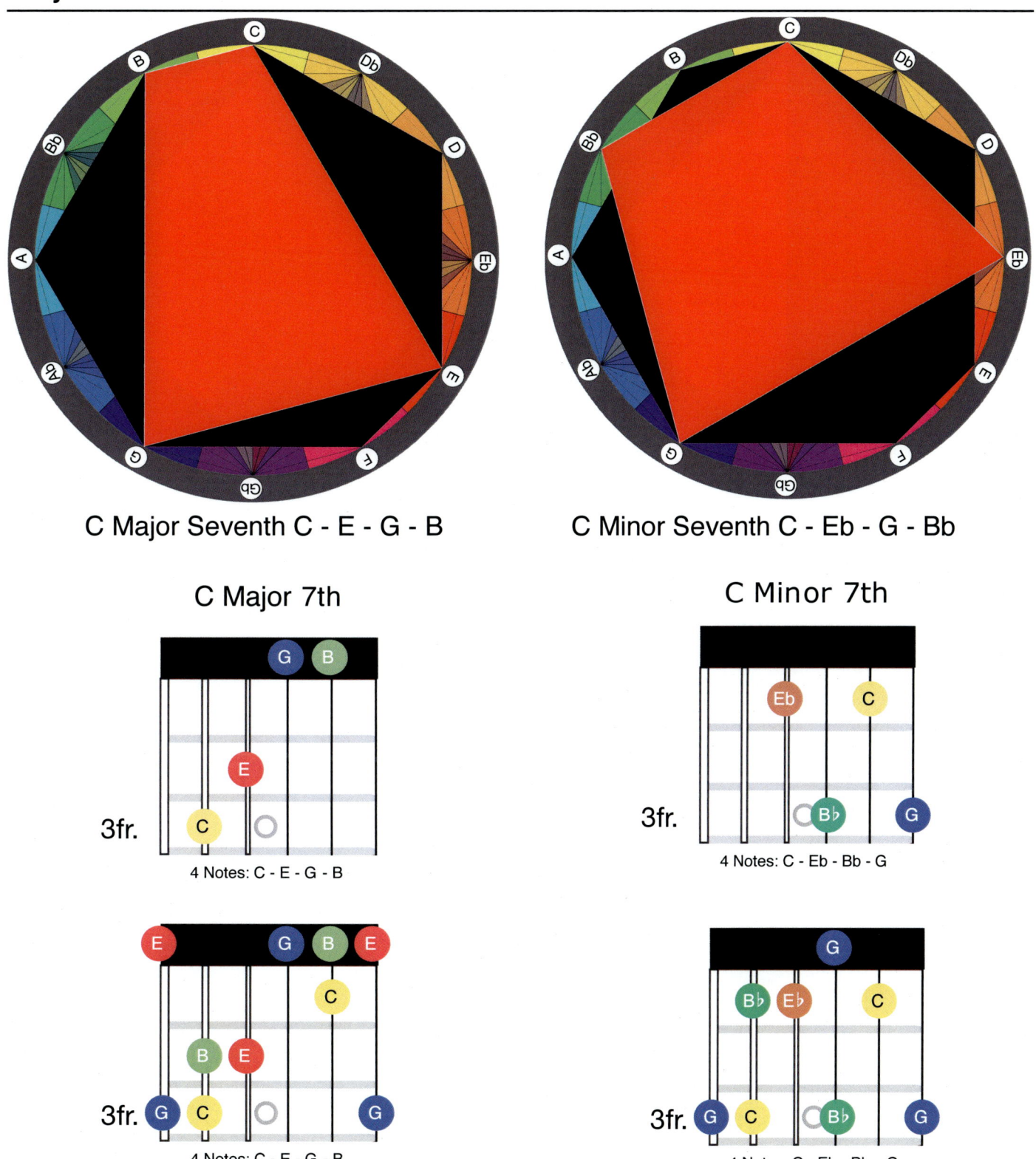

C Major Seventh C - E - G - B

C Minor Seventh C - Eb - G - Bb

C Major 7th

C Minor 7th

Fig. 45 C Major Seventh is composed of C - E - G - B. The Minor Seventh is accomplished by flatting the third and using the dominant seventh note (Bb.)

C Diminished Triad and Seventh Shapes
Diminished Triad 1 - b3 - b5 Diminished Seventh 1 - b3 - b5 - bb7

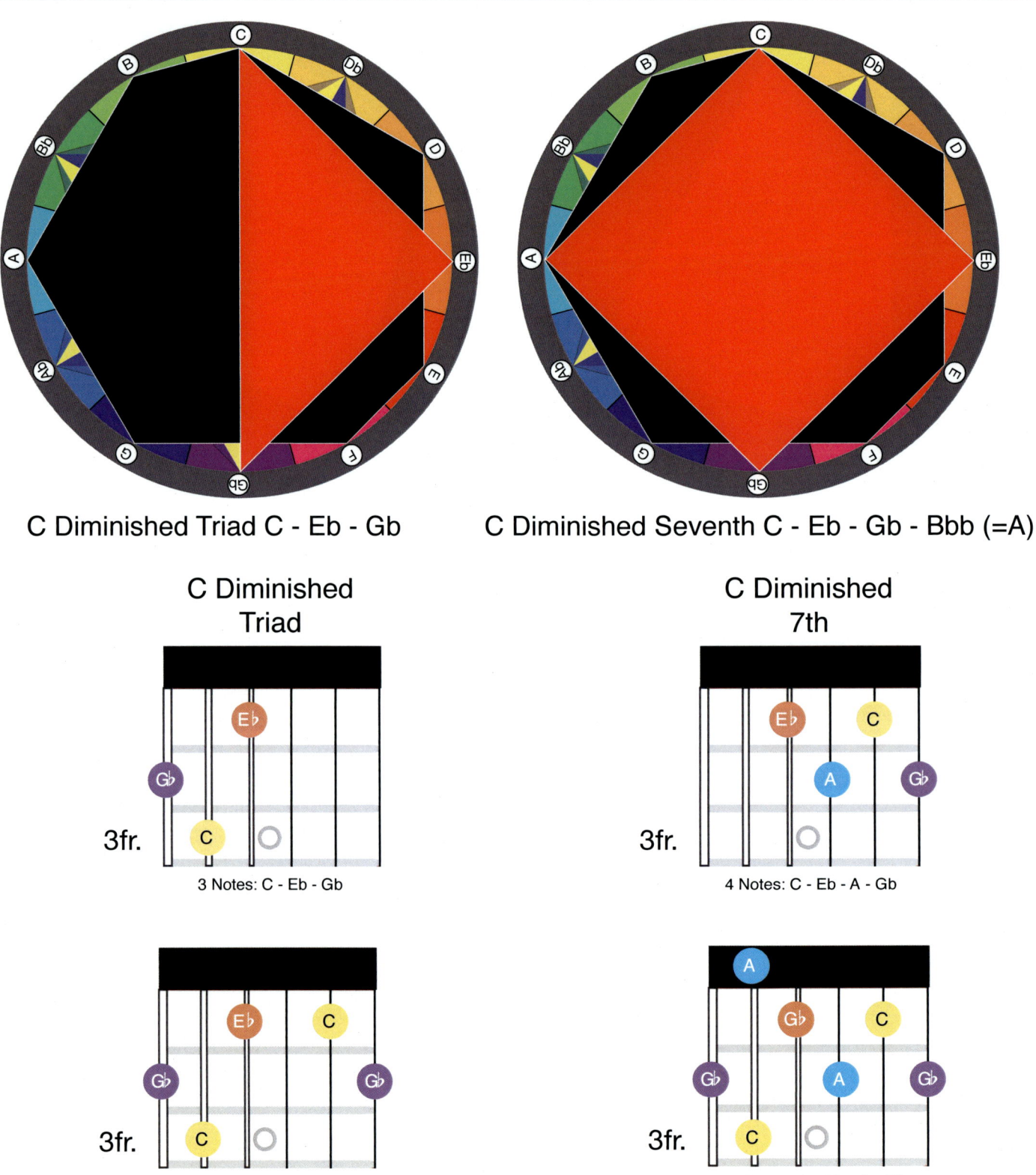

C Diminished Triad C - Eb - Gb

C Diminished Seventh C - Eb - Gb - Bbb (=A)

C Diminished
Triad

3fr.

3 Notes: C - Eb - Gb

C Diminished
7th

3fr.

4 Notes: C - Eb - A - Gb

3fr.

3 Notes: C - Eb - Gb

3fr.

4 Notes: C - Eb - A - F#

Fig. 46. Notice the symmetry: isosceles triangle with two equal sides, the square with four equal sides.

C Augmented Triad and Seventh Shapes
Augmented Triad 1 - 3 - #5 - Augmented Seventh 1 - 3 - #5 - b7

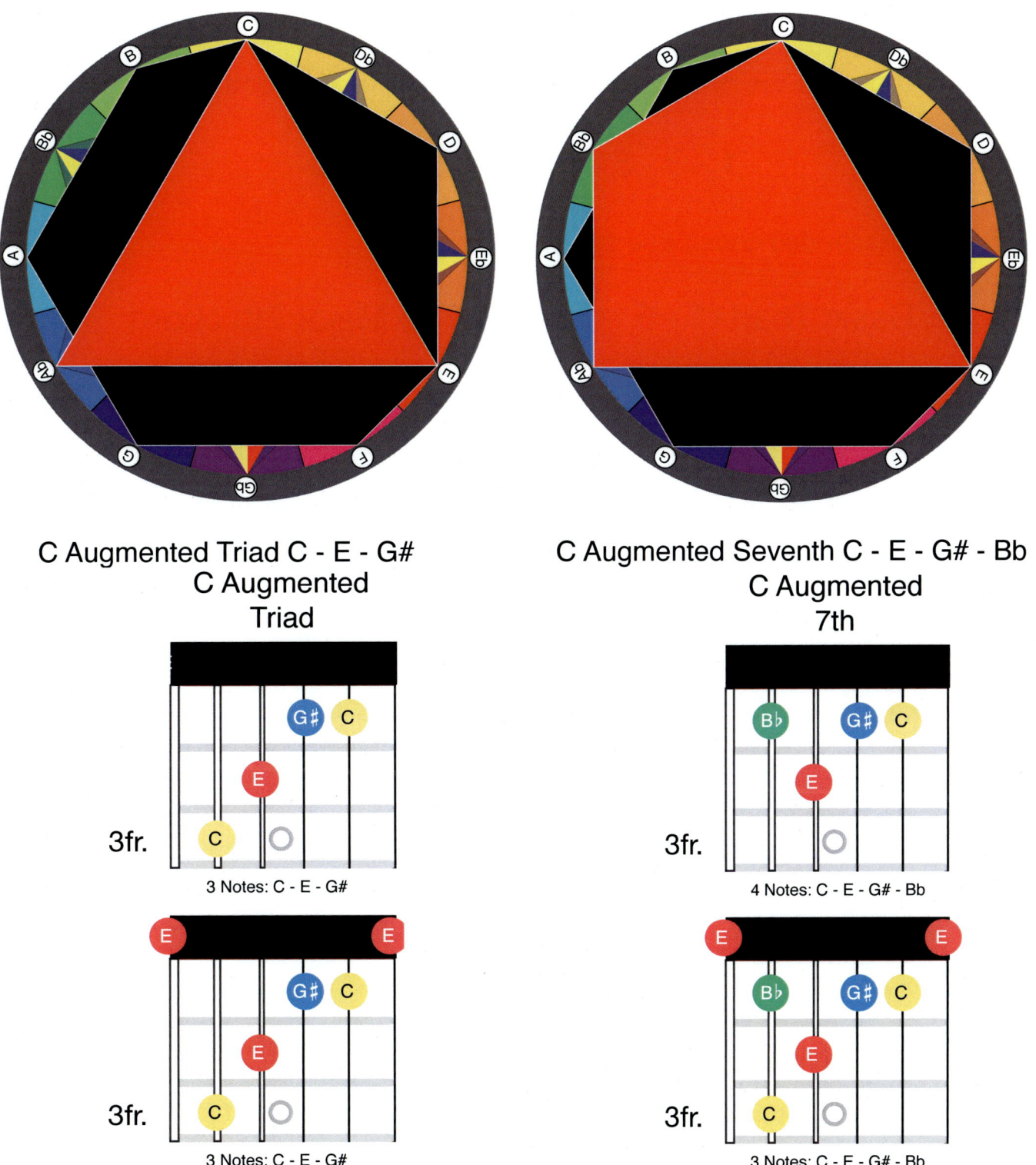

C Augmented Triad C - E - G#
C Augmented
Triad

3 Notes: C - E - G#

3 Notes: C - E - G#

C Augmented Seventh C - E - G# - Bb
C Augmented
7th

4 Notes: C - E - G# - Bb

3 Notes: C - E - G# - Bb

Fig. 47. Notice the equilateral triangle depicting the Augmented Chord and the smooth transition to the kite shape of the augmented seventh chord form.

Numbers Make Extensions

The extensions are the odd numbers found above the octave.

These are known as the ninth (9th), eleventh (11th) and thirteenth (13th).

$$1 - 3 - 5 - 7 - \mathbf{9 - 11 - 13}$$

To create an extended chord, use this formula:

Basic Triad (1 - 3 - 5) + 7 = The Major 7th chord

Then add the desired note.

Odd Numbers above the octave (eight) are derived in the following way. Start with the Major Seventh and add the notes from above the octave with the 2, 4, or 6:

Major 7 + 2 = Major 9th
Major 7 + 4 = Major 11th
Major 7 + 6 = Major 13th

To determine the essential notes and the makeup for extended chords, simply add two, four or six to the major seventh chord. The result is the: 9th, 11th or 13th.

Working the other way around, subtract seven from the extension (9th, 11th, 13th), and the result is a suspended 2 (D), 4 (F) or 6 (A), respectively. It works both ways = additive and subtractive. This results in the note names. "Sus" is the abbreviation for suspended; it represents even numbers below the octave and another way to describe a degree added to the chord.

2 - 4 - 6 - 8 - "10" - "12"

Seven is the magic number. Subtract 7 from the even numbers: 10 and 12. The remainder is either a 3 or a 5, essentially, just doubling the third and the fifth degree of the scale in the next higher register.

Odd		Odd		Odd		Odd		Odd Major
	Even		Even		Even		Even	Even Minor
1	2	3	4	5	6	7	8	Degrees(°s)
Tonic	Super Tonic	Mediant	Sub-Dominant	Dominant	Sub-Mediant	Sub-Tonic	Tonic	Function
C	D	E	F	G	A	B	C	Note Names
Ionian	Dorian	Phrygian	Lydian	Mixolydian	Aeolian	Locrian	Ionian	Mode

Fig. 48. The items on the function line are the names, regardless of the key. The names on the bottom line are the modes–recurring sound patterns, using the major scale as the template; for the notes pattern and spacings. Each modal pattern begins on a respective degree and follows the same spacing pattern of major scale.

1	2	3	4	5	6	7	8	9	10	11	12	13	(°s)
C	D	E	F	G	A	B	C	D	E	F	G	A	Name
Odd		Odd		Odd		Odd		X		X		X	Odd Major
	Even		Even		Even		Even		X		X		Even Minor
1	2	3	4	5	6	7	8	9	10	11	12	13	(°s)

Fig. 49. Notes above the octave are known as extensions indicated by the X's in the teal-colored boxes; the two, four, six added to the seventh chord become the ninth, eleventh and thirteenth.

Extensions are added after the first octave range (to the right of the red rectangle). These are the odd numbers above the octave known as the ninth, eleventh and thirteenth degrees.

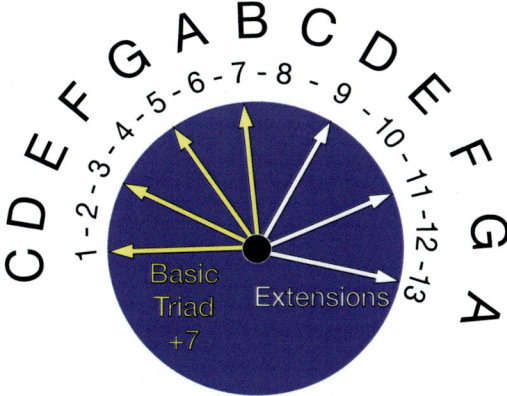

Fig. 50. The odd numbers above the octave are the 9,11 and 13 and are a repeat of the 2 - 4 - 6 and correspond to the notes: D - F - A. Above the octave, even numbers convert to odd numbers. The polarities change from major to minor, and vice versa. The even numbers above the octave are duplicate components of the Basic Triad: C = 1 and/or 8: E = 3 and/or 10: G = 5 and/or 12.

Numbers in Chords - Based on the Major Scale

Basic Triad						Extensions start and build above the seventh degree - add 2, 4, or 6							Descriptor Name
1	2	3	4	5	6	7	8	9	10	11	12	13	(°) Degree
C	D	E	F	G	A	B	C	D	E	F	G	A	Letters / Name
C	D	E	F	G	A	B	C						Major Scale
1		3		5									Basic Triad
1		3		5		7							Major 7 Chord
1	2	3		5		7		9					Major 9
1		3	4	5		7				11			Major 11
1		3		5	6	7						13	Major 13
C	D	E	F	G	A	B	C	D	E	F	G	A	Letter
1	2	3	4	5	6	7	8	9	10	11	12	13	Number

Fig. 51. Referring to the two bottom rows for reference–letters and numbers: D equals both the two and the nine. Notice how the letters on the scale repeat. The Red Column is the seventh–the dividing line–the halfway transition point. The beginning of the extensions:

Major 7 + 2 = Major 9 = D (two = nine = D)
Major 7 + 4 = Major 11 = F (four = eleven = F)
Major 7 + 6 = Major 13 = A (six = thirteen = A)

When adding the two, four or six to the basic triad, it is known as suspended two, four or six. When added to and above the major seventh chord, it becomes an extension. Start with the seventh chord as the basis from which to build:

Add the two (D) note to the C major seventh chord arrive at the C9 chord (C Ninth)

Add the fourth (F) note to the C major seventh chord arrive at C11 chord (C Eleventh)

Add the sixth (A) note to the C major seventh chord arrive at C13 chord (C Thirteenth)

The seventh–the leading tone–is a magical note, space and place. Basic triads are to the left of the halfway point–the seven. Seven is halfway between one and thirteen, represented by the red boxes. The extensions are to the right, starting at eight, spanning through thirteen. Moving up the scale after the seven note, the polarity changes—odd becomes even and even becomes odd. Remember: when using the major scale, the seventh is the leading and last note before the octave and the beginning of a higher register.

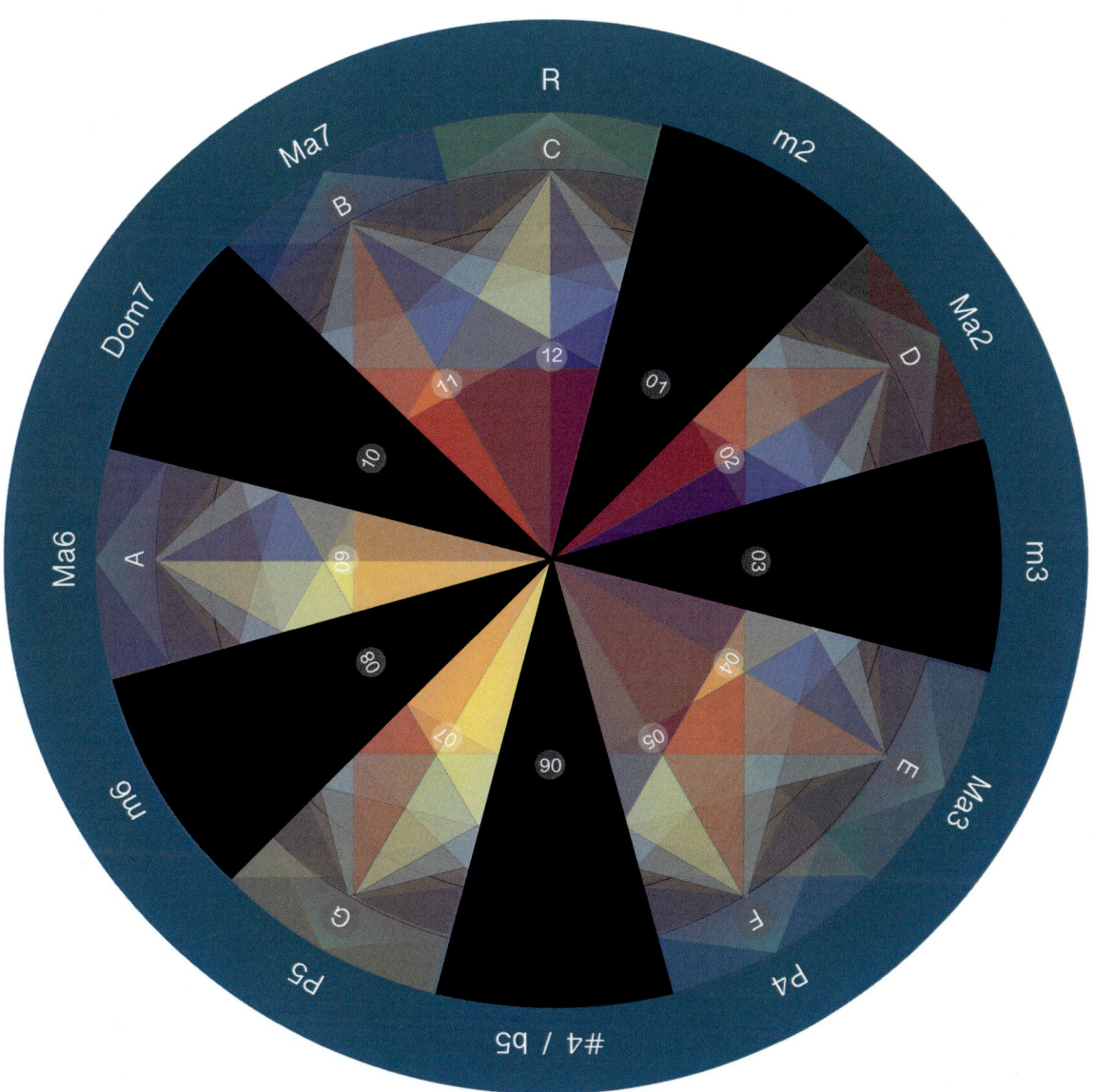

Fig. 52. This graphic represents the C major scale. This graphic helps identify the notes found in the C major, arpeggio, extensions, scales, chords and progressions. The 01, 03, 06, 08, and 10 o'clock positions (m2, m3, #4/b5, m6, Dom7) are darkened and represent the accidental notes designated by a flat (b) or a sharp (#). Drop or ignore the darkened slices from the chromatic to form the C major scale: C - D - E - F - G - A - B - C, which corresponds to the 12 - 2 - 4 - 5 - 7 - 9 - 11 o'clock positions. The outside scale is described with intervals.

KEYS, CODES and MODES

Orientation - 12 Major Scales
Chromatic Orientation

The following visuals provide tools for understanding the big picture and navigating through the 12 keys. Shapes and symbols rotate around the center point of the circle and reveal note arrangements. Superimposed stencils and masks highlight important and recurring patterns. This demonstrates corresponding patterns found in the keys, scales, chords and arpeggios.

The C note closest to the "eye" near the center is the starting point for the notes of the **ascending** scale.

The C note closest to the outside–circumference–is the starting point for the notes of the **descending** scale.

The following pages demonstrate each of the major scales in the 12 keys and relational locations. This is the constellation of major scales and arranged in the ascending clockwise chromatic order.

The fretboard patterns are offered as notes and intervals based in the key of C. These are chords, arpeggios and scales. The graphic on the bottom is the complete fretboard displayed in intervals.

12 o'clock position
C Major Scale - Chromatic Orientation

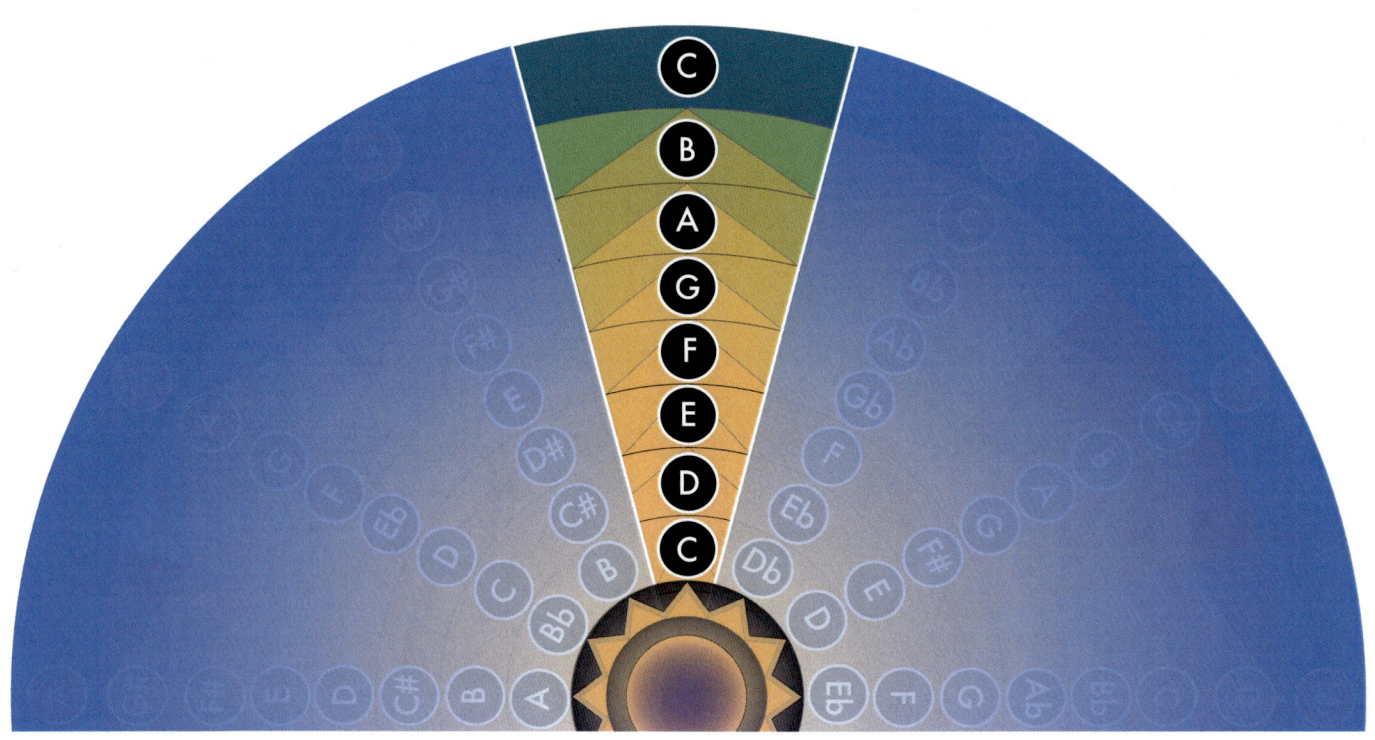

C Major Key
Number of Sharps/Flats = 0 (no Flats / no Sharps)
C - D - E - F - G - A - B - C
1 - 2 - 3 - 4 - 5 - 6 - 7 - 8
C - B - A - G - F - E - D - C

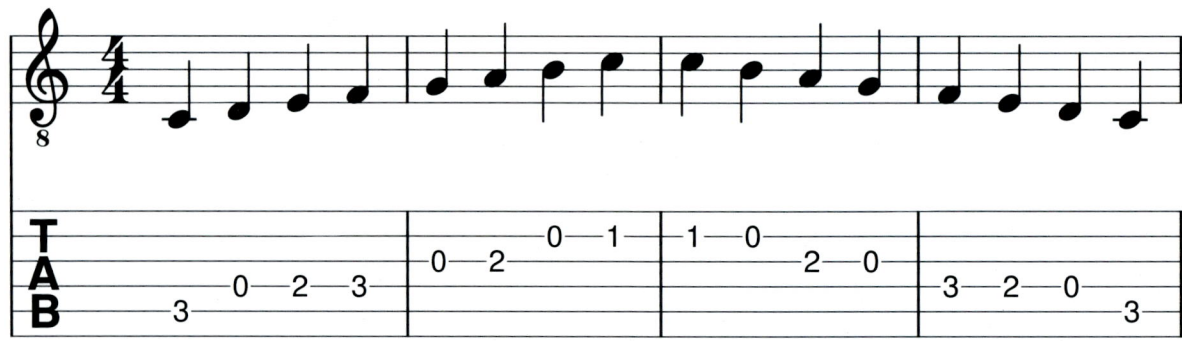

Fig. 53. C Major Key viewed in multiple formats - graphic, alphanumerics, staff/tab.

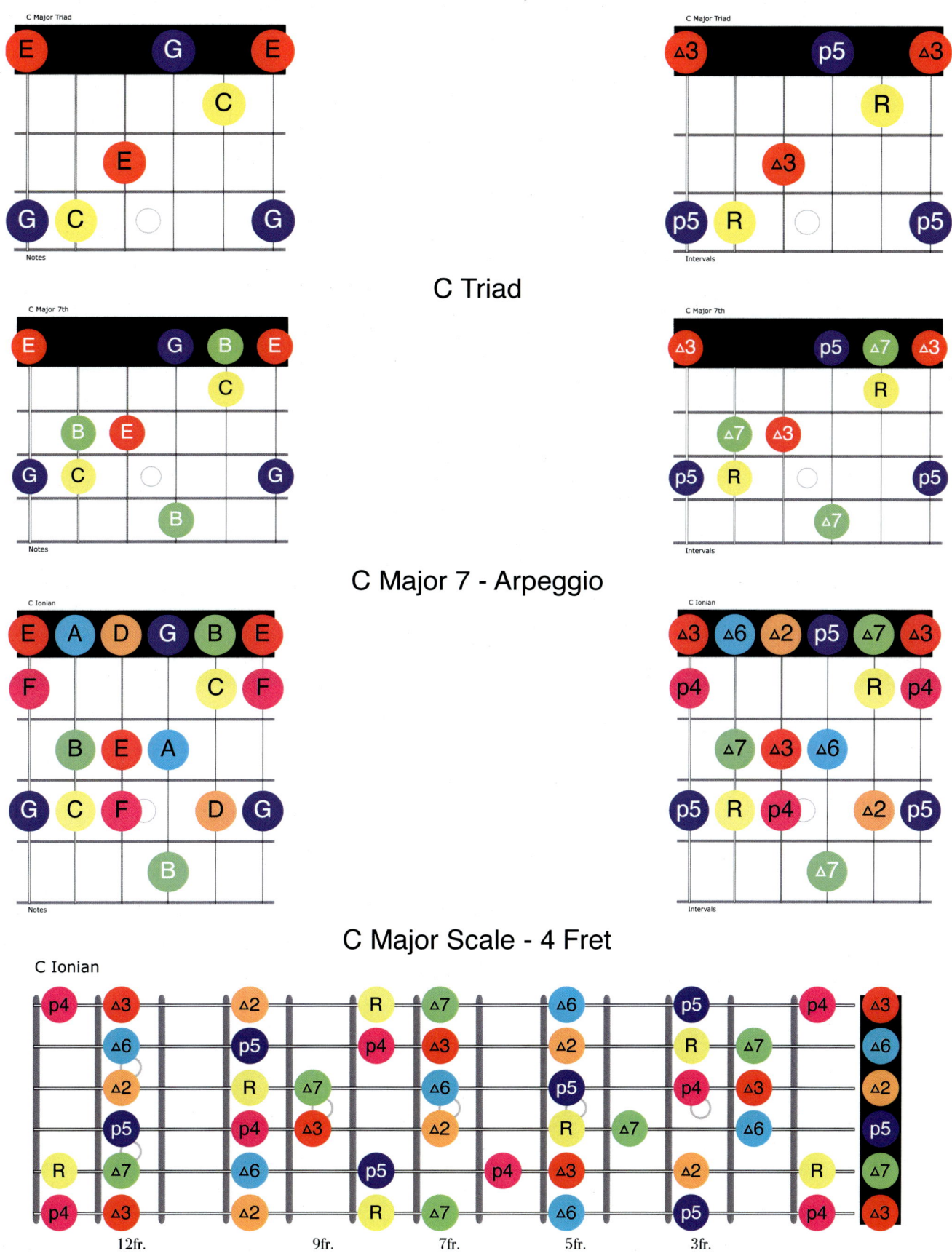

C Triad

C Major 7 - Arpeggio

C Major Scale - 4 Fret

C Major Scale - 12 Fret

Fig. 54. C Major Key - representation of fretboard with notes and intervals.

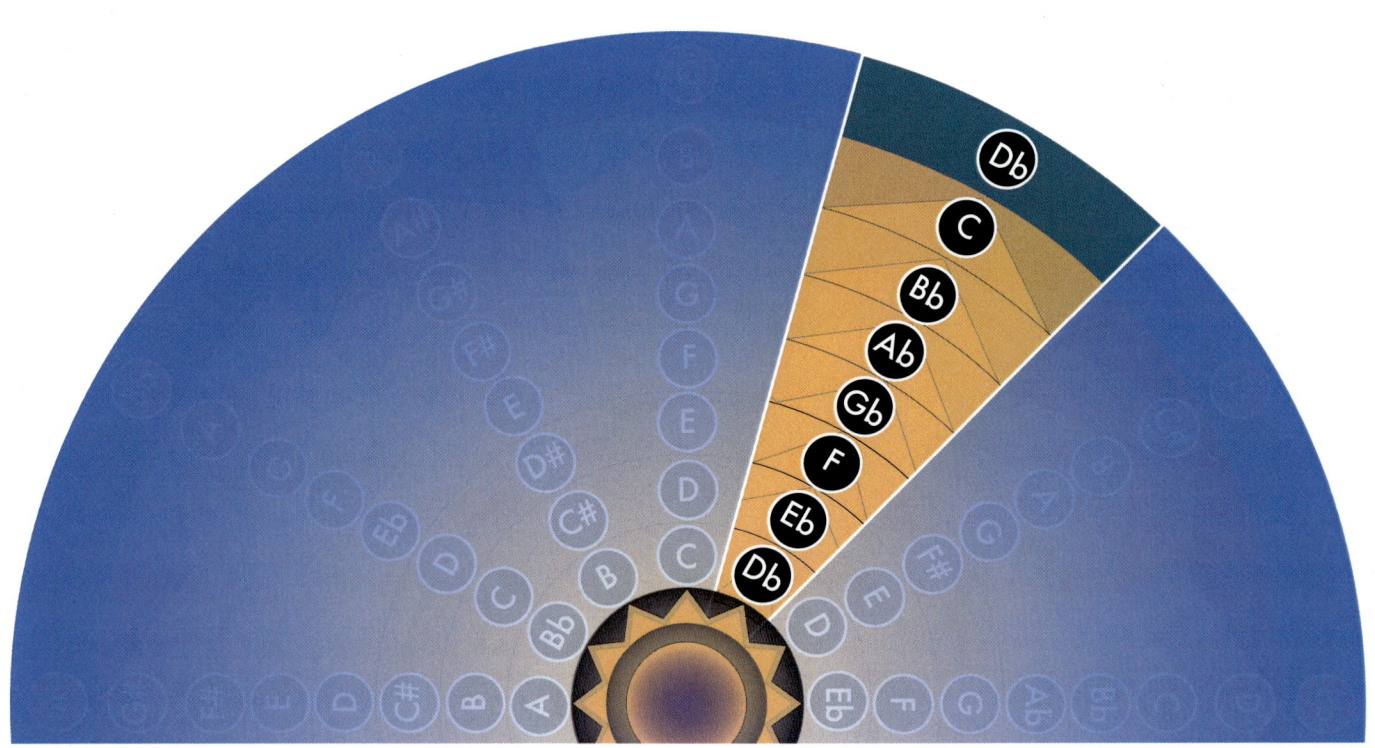

Db Major Key
Number of Sharps/Flats = 5 Flats (Db / Eb / Gb / Ab / Bb)
Db - Eb - F - Gb - Ab - Bb - C - Db
1 - 2 - 3 - 4 - 5 - 6 - 7 - 8
Db - C - Bb - Ab - Gb - F - Eb - Db

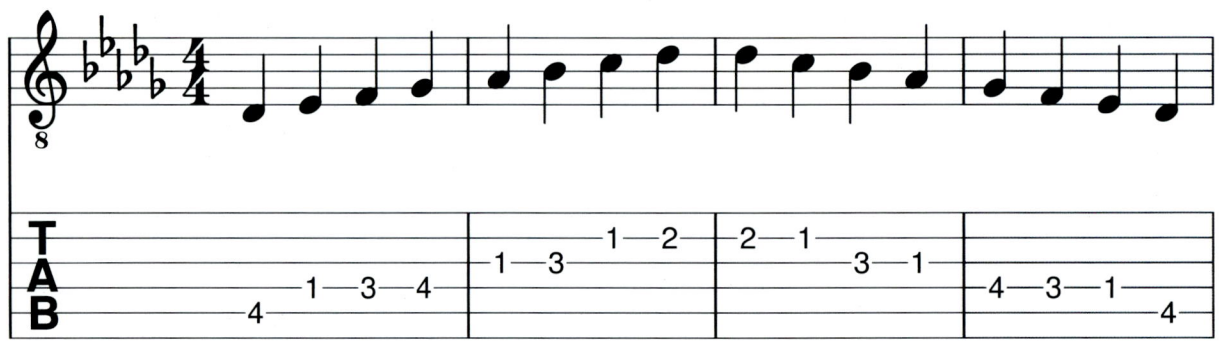

Fig. 55. Db Major Key viewed in multiple formats - graphic, alphanumerics, staff/tab.

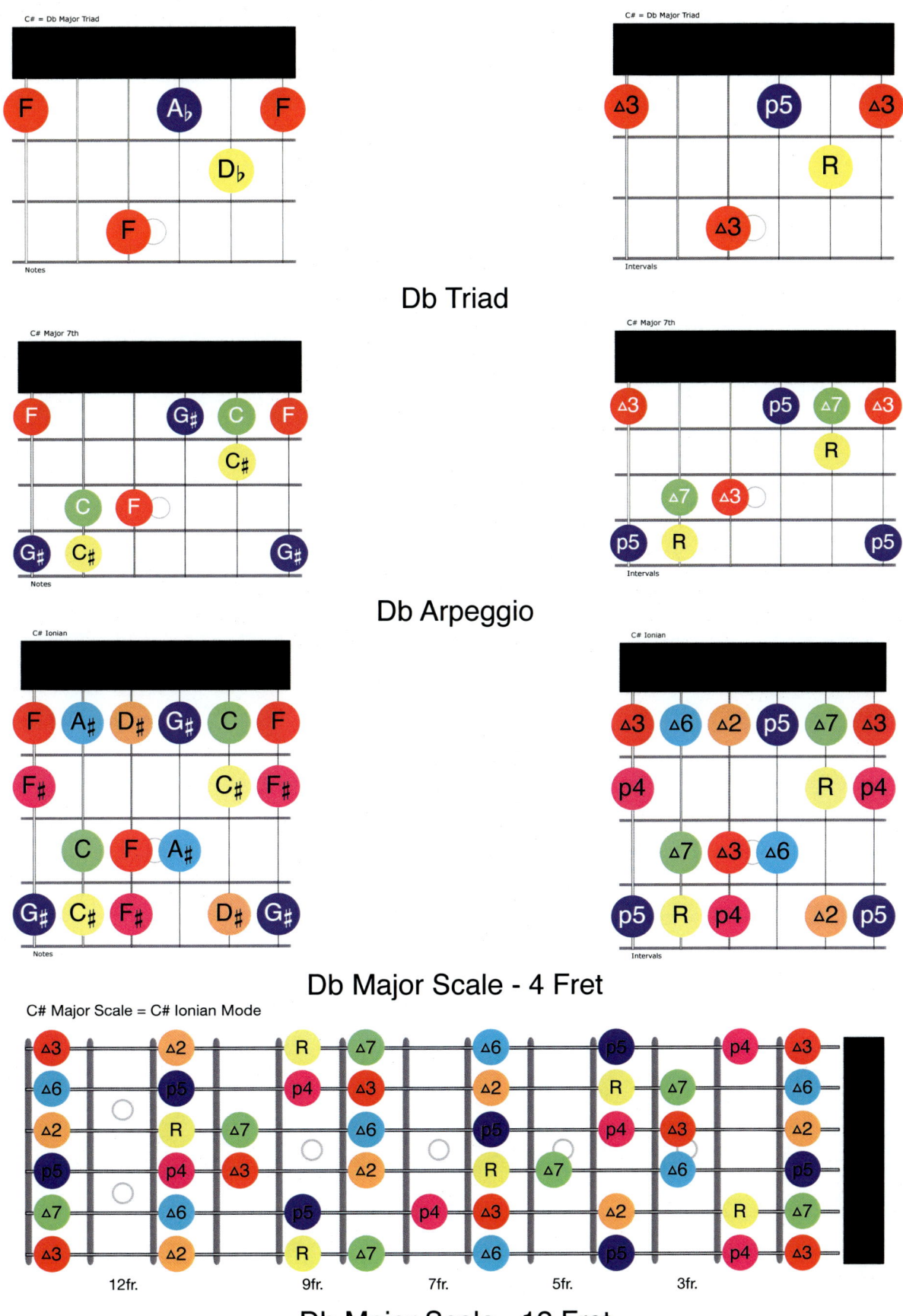

Db Triad

Db Arpeggio

Db Major Scale - 4 Fret

Db Major Scale - 12 Fret

Fig. 56. Db Major Key - representation of fretboard with notes and intervals.

D Major Scale - Chromatic Orientation

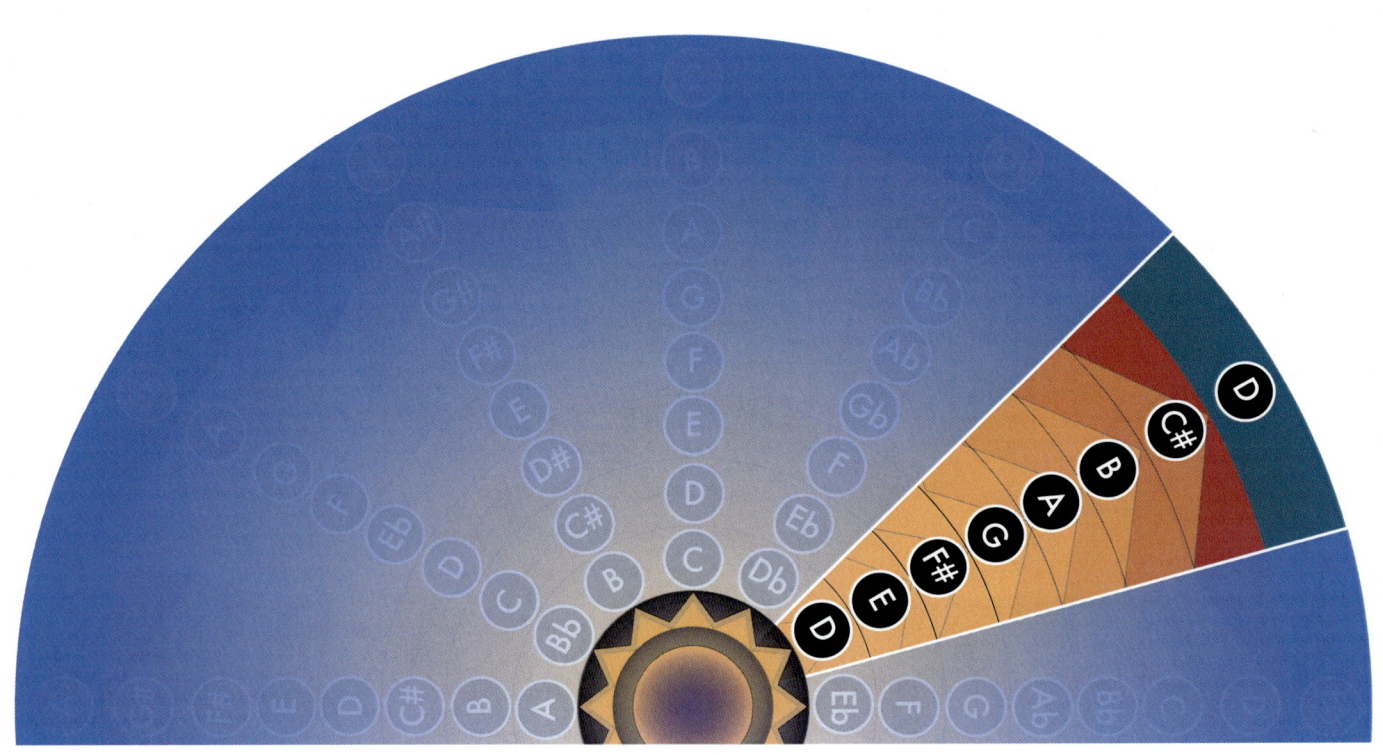

D Major Key
Number of Sharps/Flats = 2 Sharps (F# / C#)
D - E - F# - G - A - B - C# - D
1 - 2 - 3 - 4 - 5 - 6 - 7 - 8
D - C# - B - A - G - F# - E - D

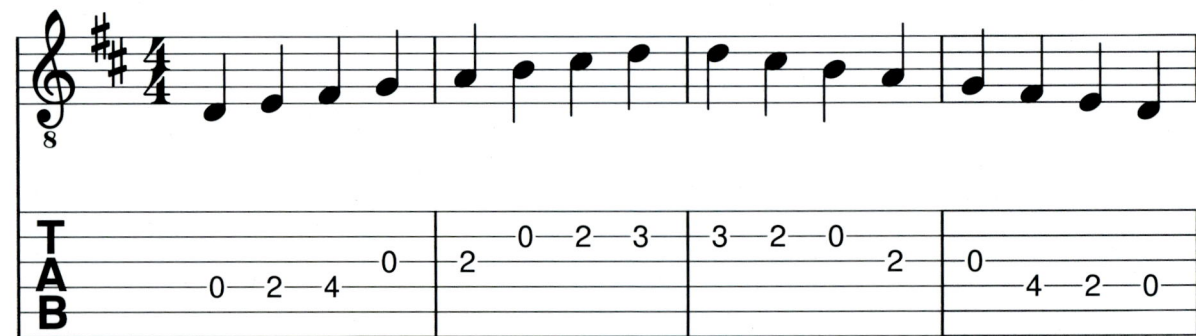

Fig. 57. D Major Key viewed in multiple formats - graphic, alphanumerics, staff/tab.

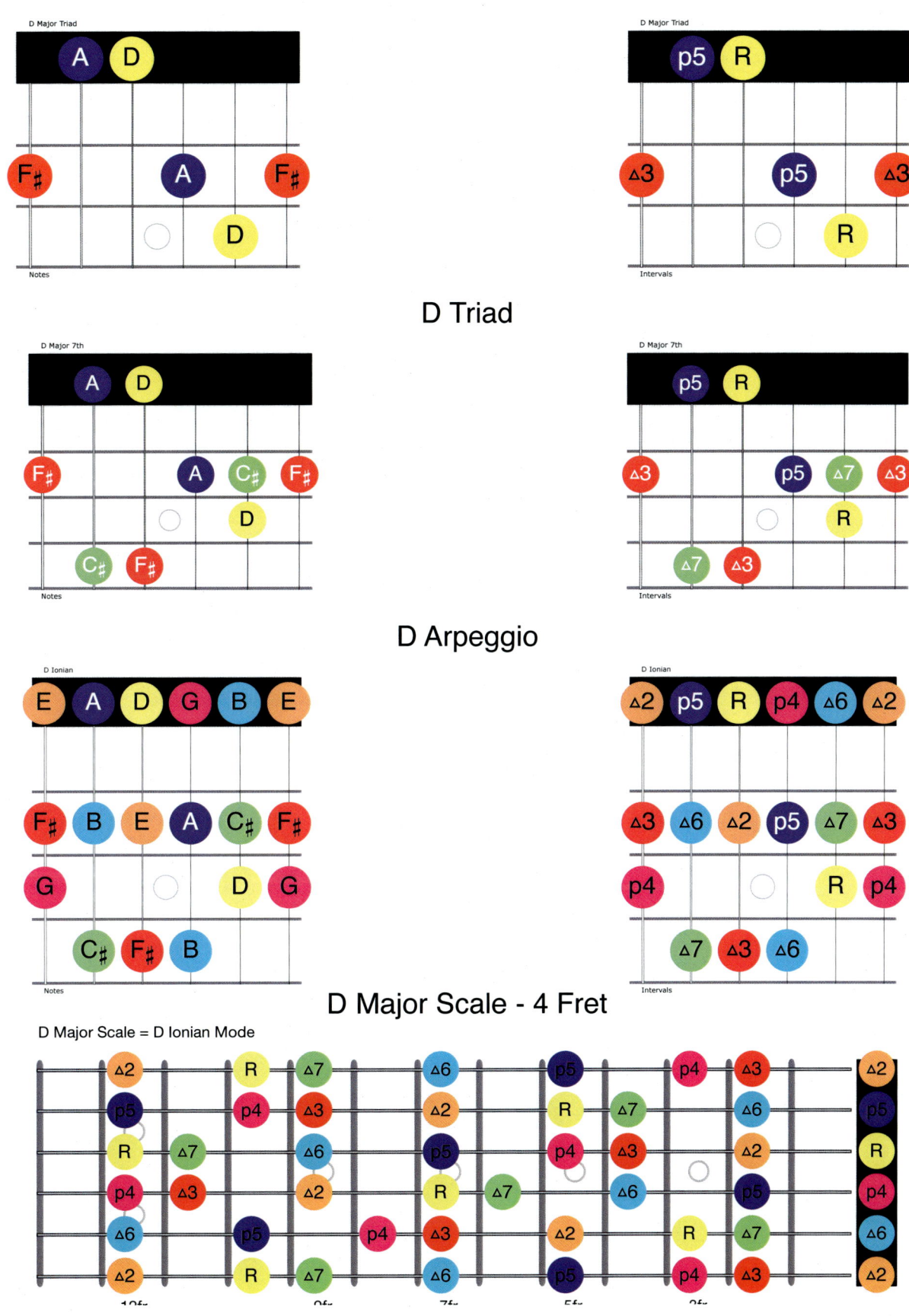

D Triad

D Arpeggio

D Major Scale - 4 Fret

D Major Scale - 12 Fret

Fig. 58. D Major Key - representation of fretboard with notes and intervals.

3 o'clock position
Eb Major Scale - Chromatic Orientation

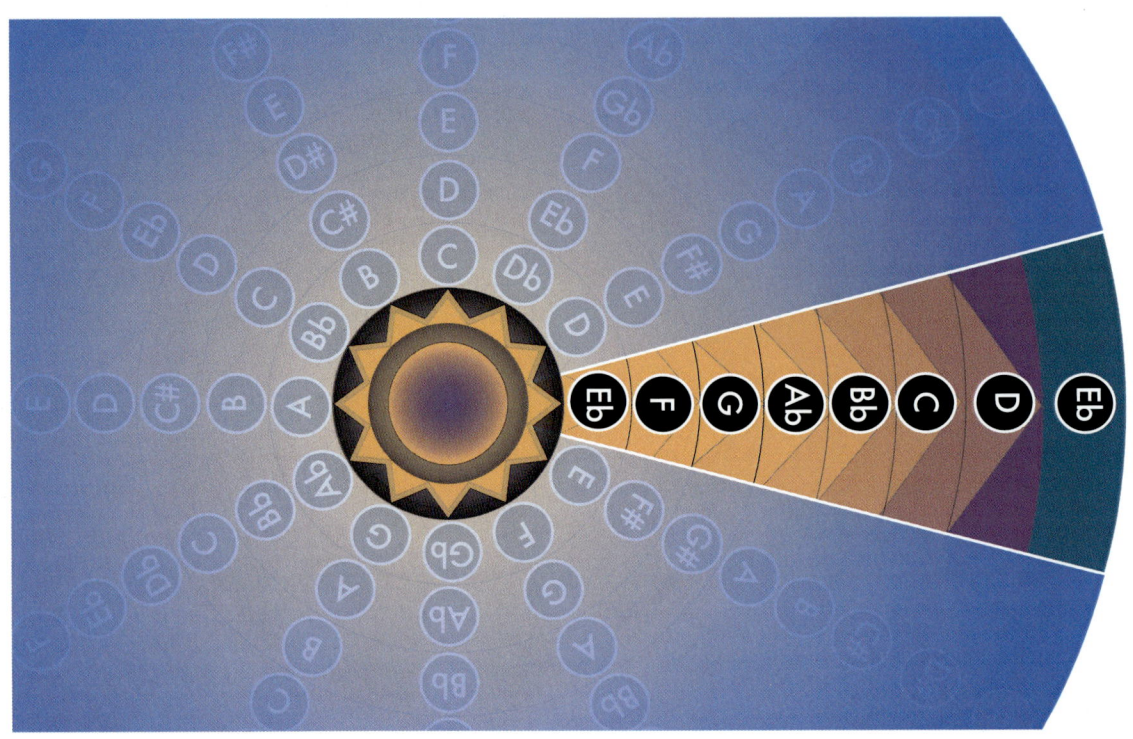

Eb Major Key
Number of Sharps/Flats = 3 Flats (Bb / Eb / Ab)
Eb - F - G - A - Bb - C - D - Eb
1 - 2 - 3 - 4 - 5 - 6 - 7 - 8
Eb - D - C - Bb - A - G - F - Eb

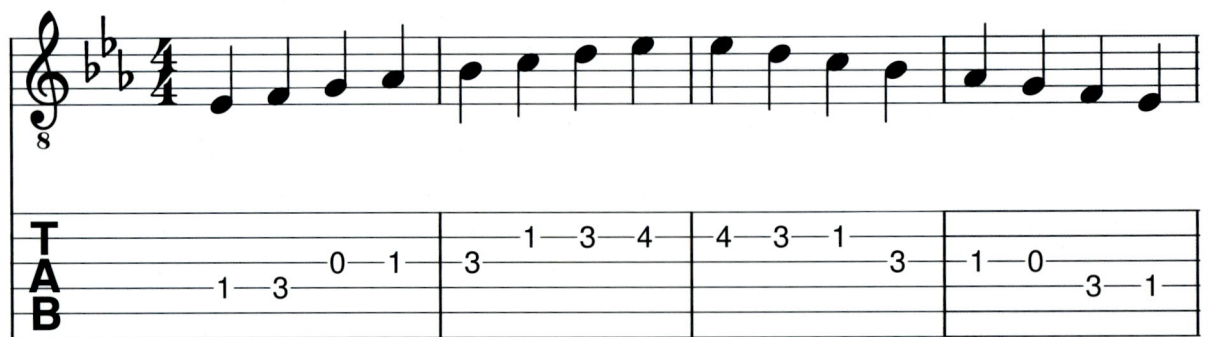

Fig. 59. Eb Major Key viewed in multiple formats - graphic, alphanumerics, staff/tab.

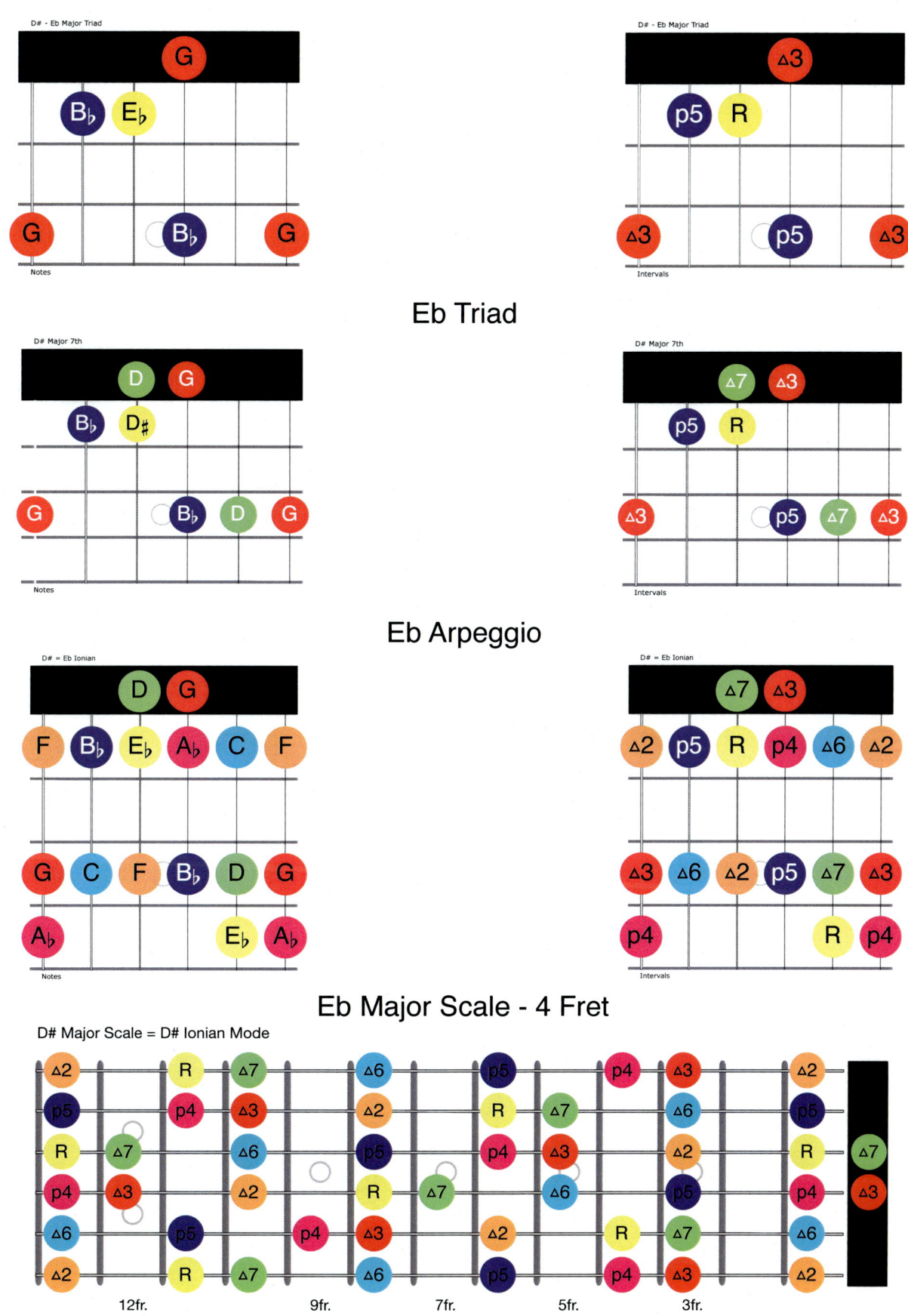

Eb Triad

Eb Arpeggio

Eb Major Scale - 4 Fret

Eb Major Scale - 12 Fret

Fig. 60. Eb Major Key - representation of fretboard with notes and intervals.

4 o'clock position
E Major Scale - Chromatic Orientation

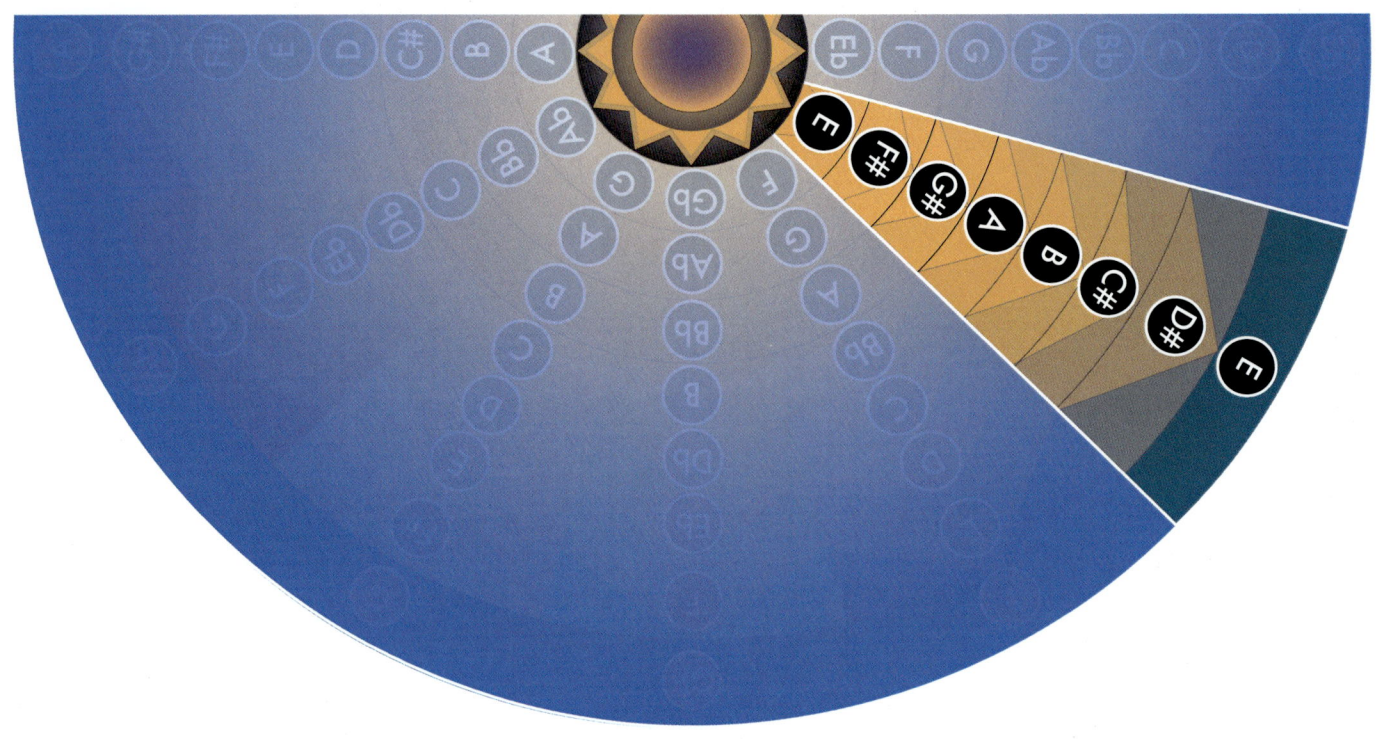

E Major Key
Number of Sharps/Flats = 4 Sharps (F# / C# / G# / D#)
E - F# - G# - A - B - C# - D# - E
1 - 2 - 3 - 4 - 5 - 6 - 7 - 8
D - D# - C# - B - A - G# - F# - D

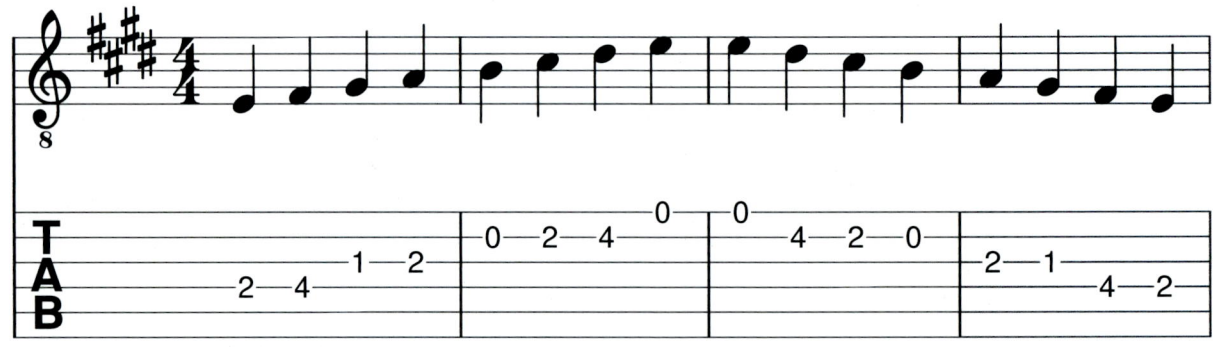

Fig. 61. E Major Key viewed in multiple formats - graphic, alphanumerics, staff/tab.

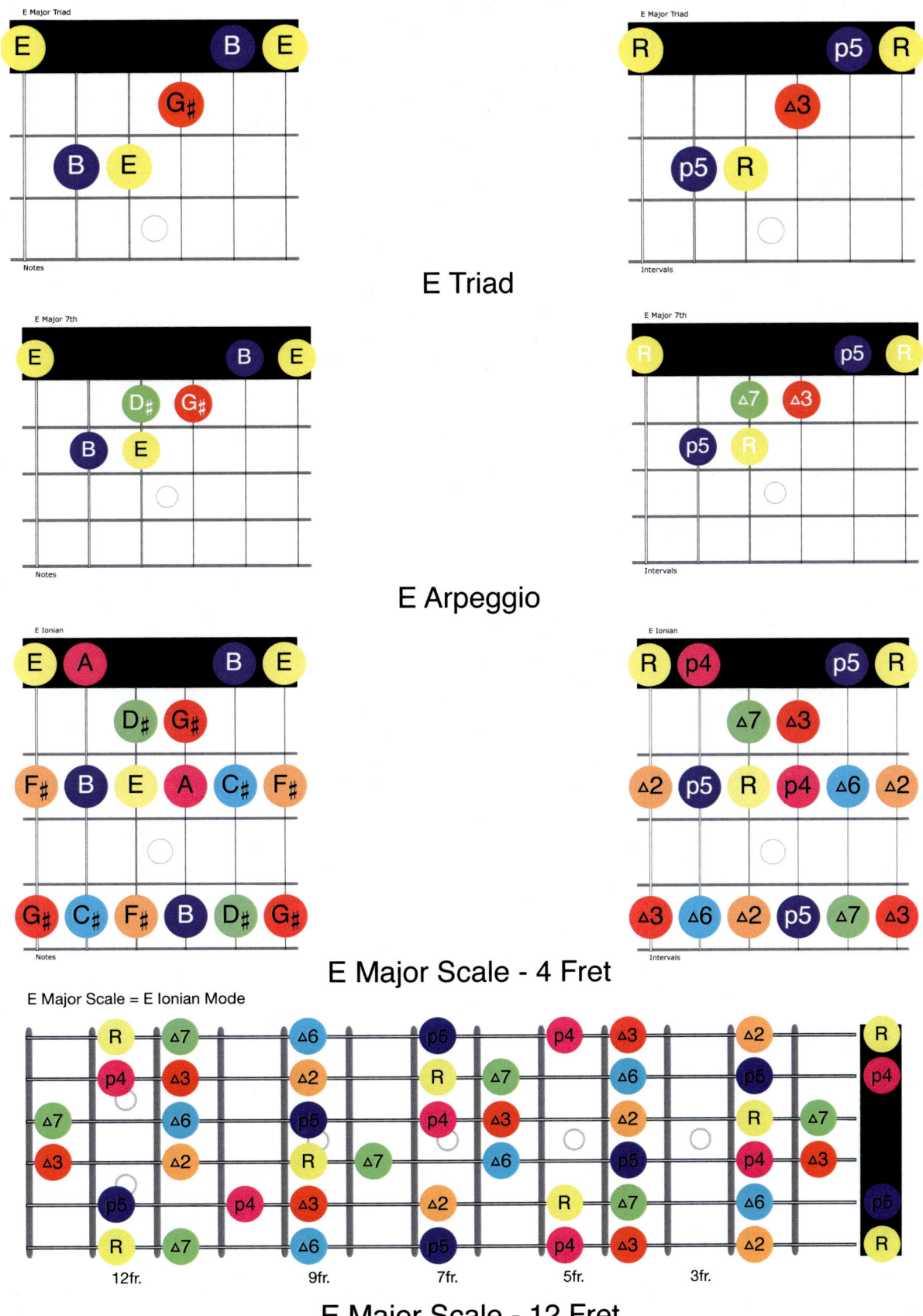

E Triad

E Arpeggio

E Major Scale - 4 Fret

E Major Scale - 12 Fret

Fig. 62. E Major Key - representation of fretboard with notes and intervals.

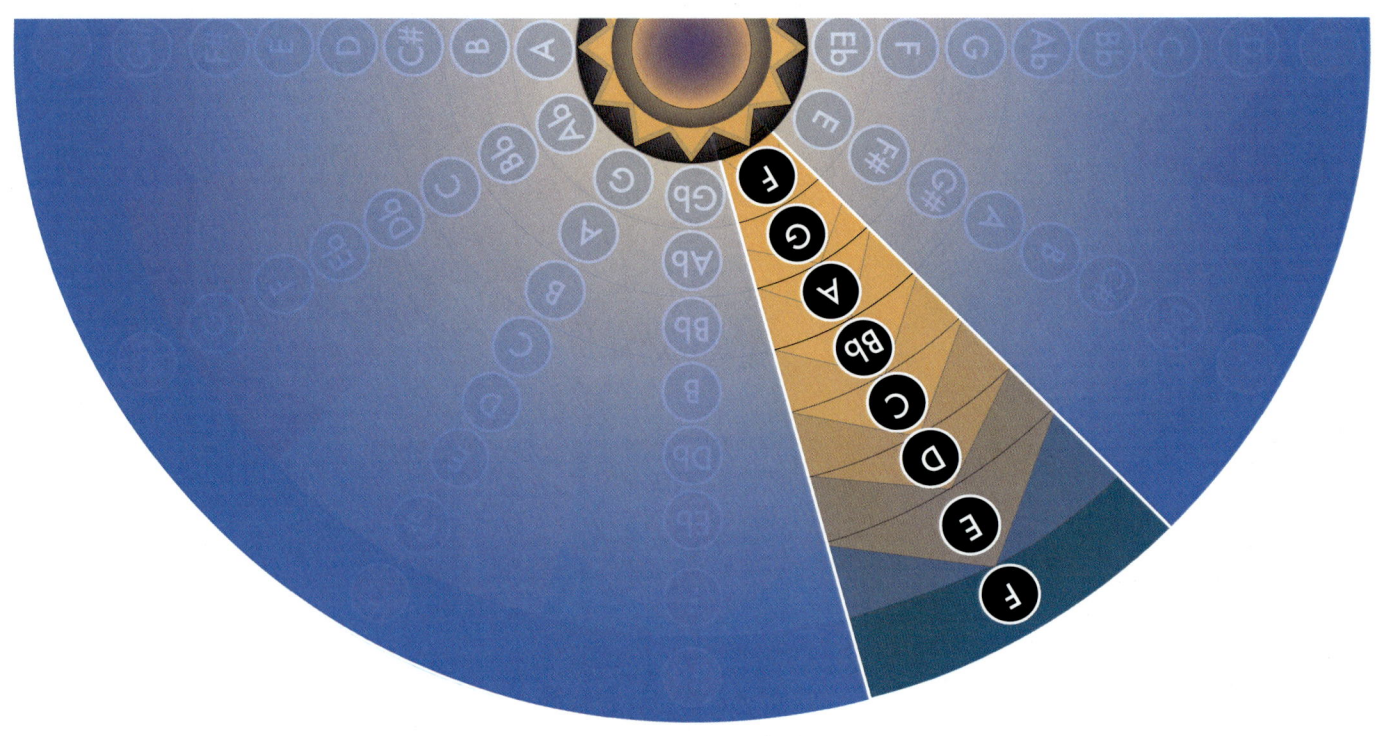

F Major Key
Number of Sharps/Flats = 1 Flat (Bb)
F - G - A - Bb - C - D - E - F
1 - 2 - 3 - 4 - 5 - 6 - 7 - 8
F - E - D - C - Bb - A - G - F

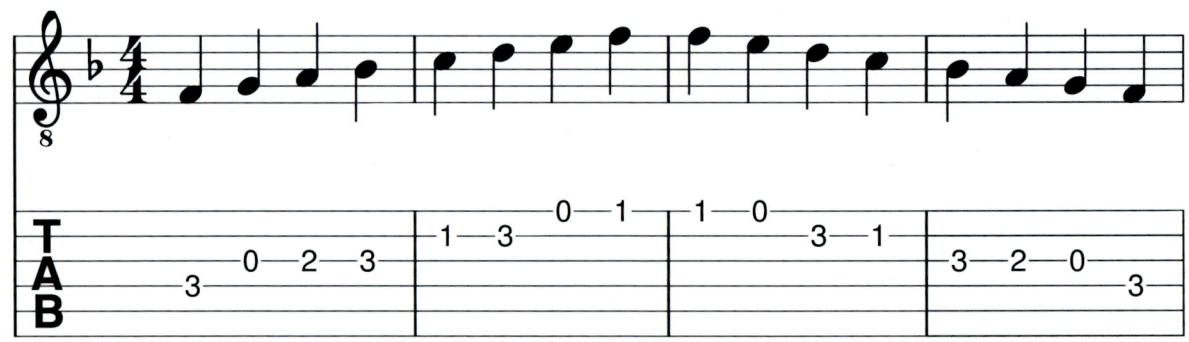

Fig. 63. F Major Key viewed in multiple formats - graphic, alphanumerics, staff/tab.

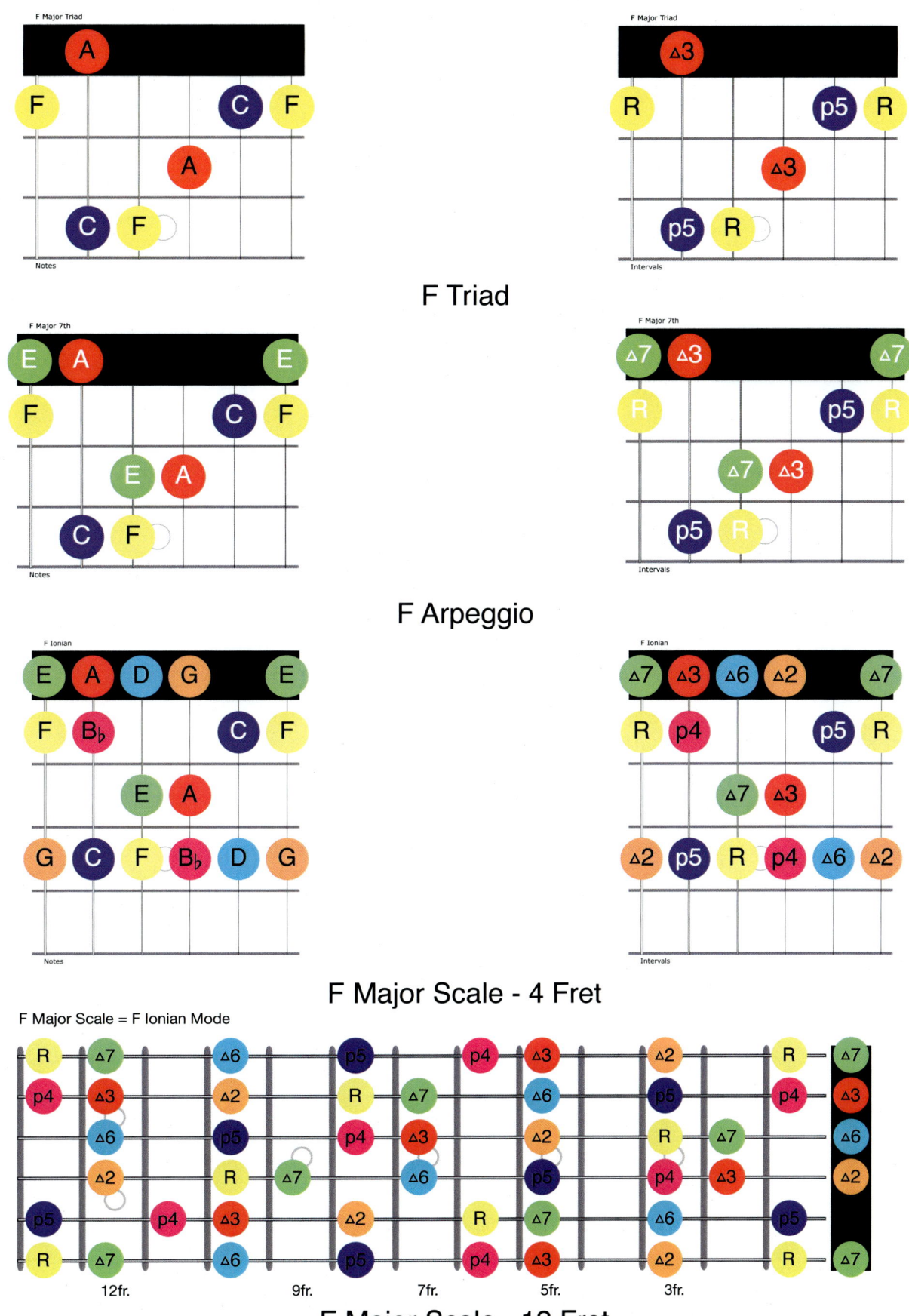

F Triad

F Arpeggio

F Major Scale - 4 Fret

F Major Scale = F Ionian Mode

F Major Scale - 12 Fret

Fig. 64. F Major Key - representation of fretboard with notes and intervals.

6 o'clock position
Gb Major Scale - Chromatic Orientation

Gb Major Key
Number of Sharps/Flats =
6 Flats (Gb / Ab / Bb / Cb = B / Db / Eb)
Gb - Ab - Bb - Cb=B - Db - Eb - F - Gb
1 - 2 - 3 - 4 - 5 - 6 - 7 - 8
Gb - F - Eb - Db - Cb=b - Bb - Ab - Gb

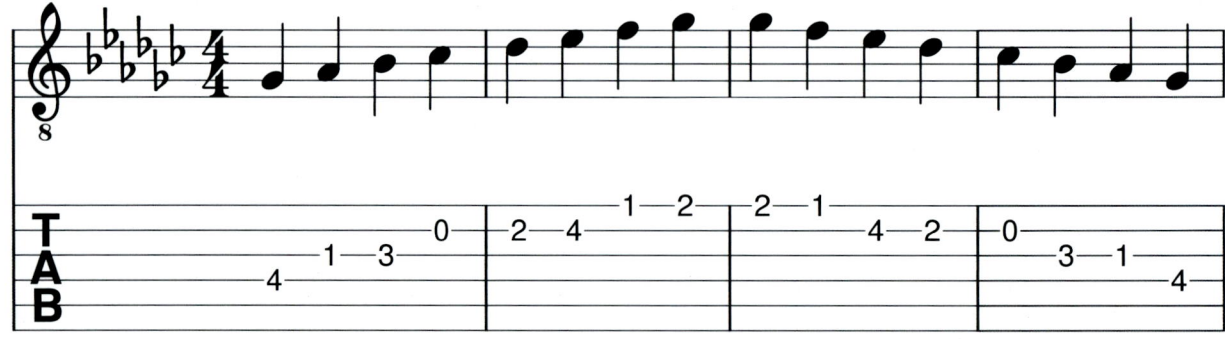

Fig. 65. Gb Major Key viewed in multiple formats - graphic, alphanumerics, staff/tab.

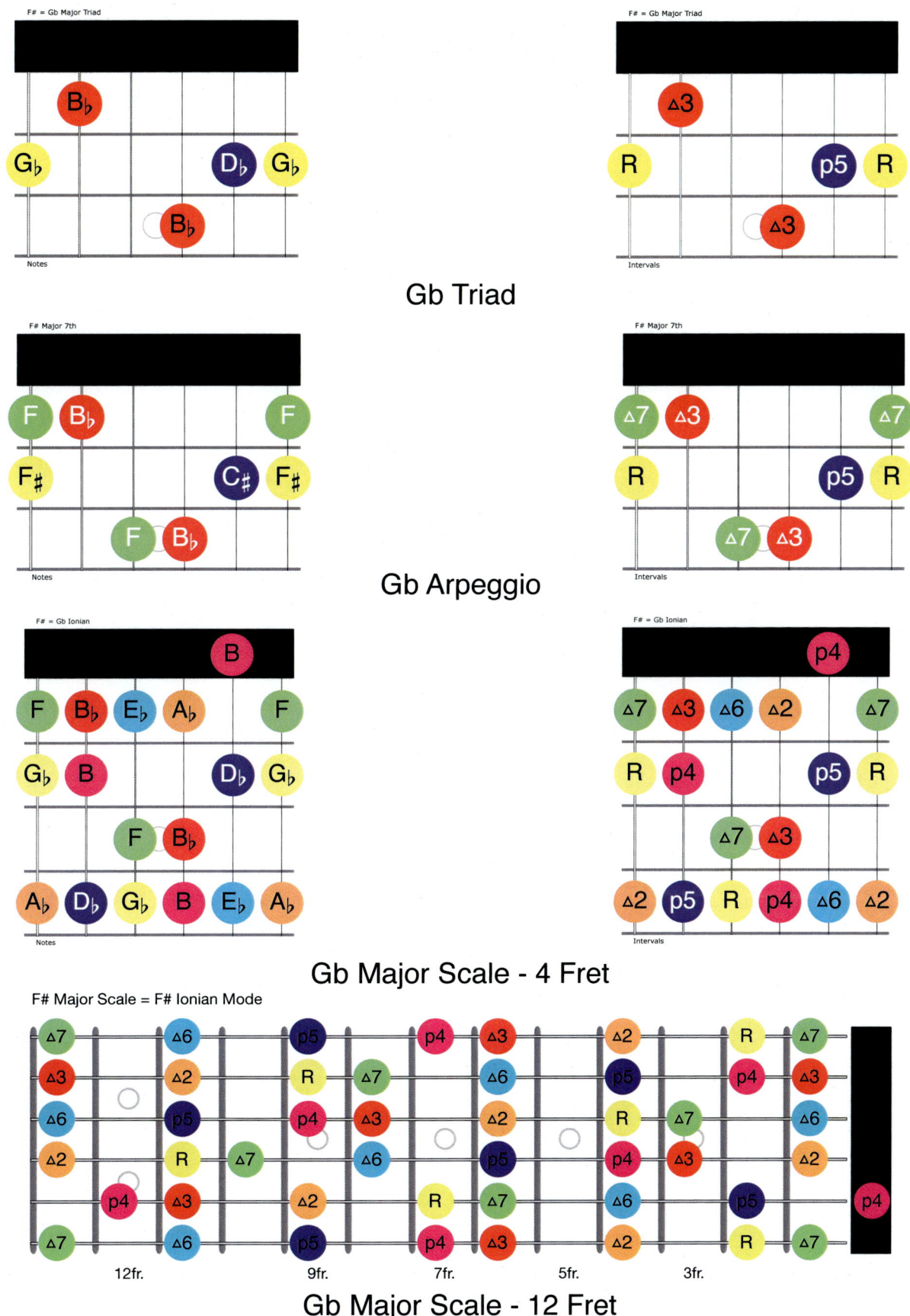

Gb Triad

Gb Arpeggio

Gb Major Scale - 4 Fret

Gb Major Scale - 12 Fret

Fig. 66. Gb Major Key - representation of fretboard with notes and intervals.

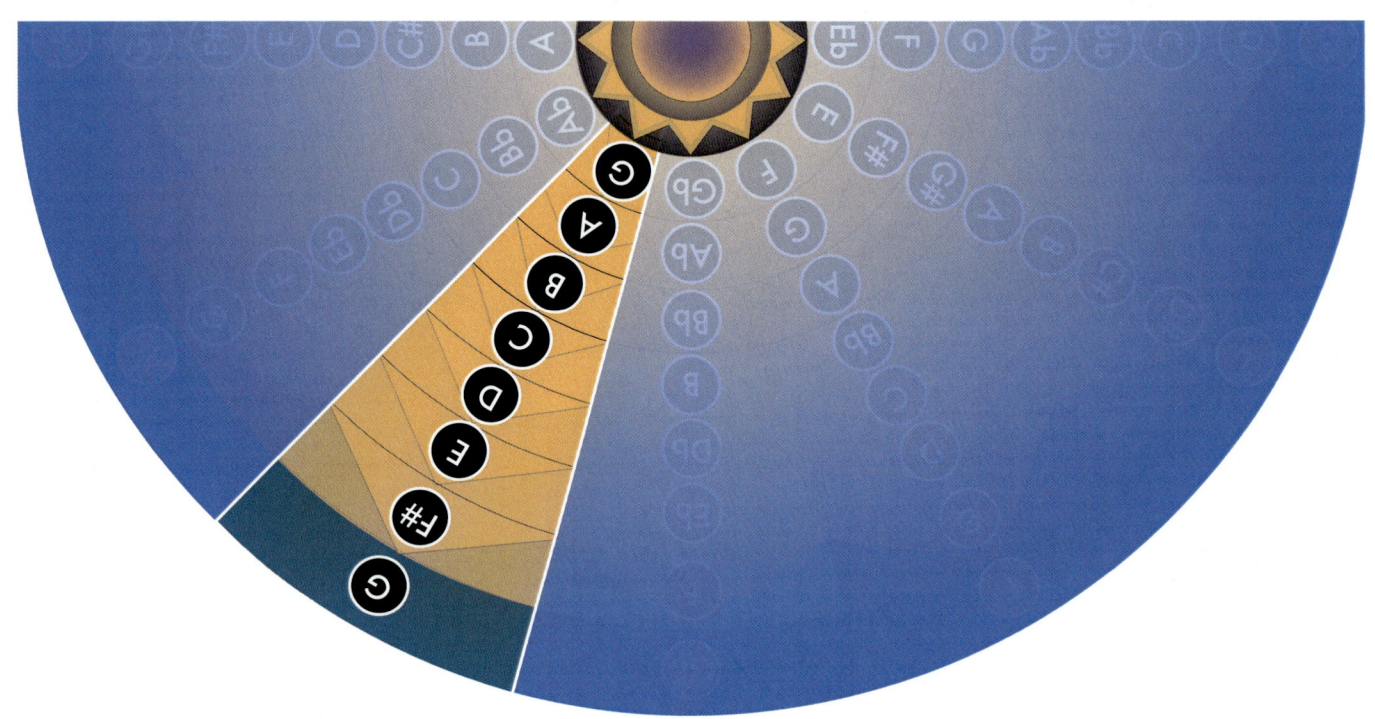

G Major Key
Number of Sharps/Flats = 1 Sharp (F#)
G - A - B - C - D - E - F# - G
1 - 2 - 3 - 4 - 5 - 6 - 7 - 8
G - F# - E - D - C - B - A - G

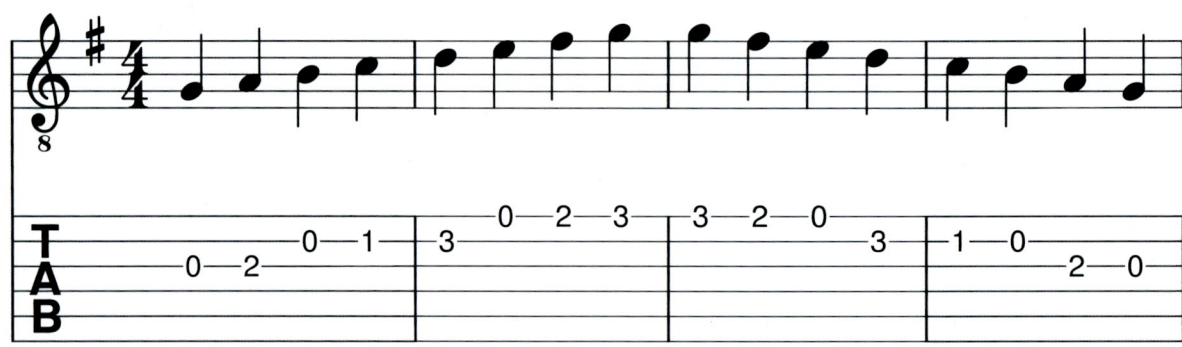

Fig. 67. G Major Key viewed in multiple formats - graphic, alphanumerics, staff/tab.

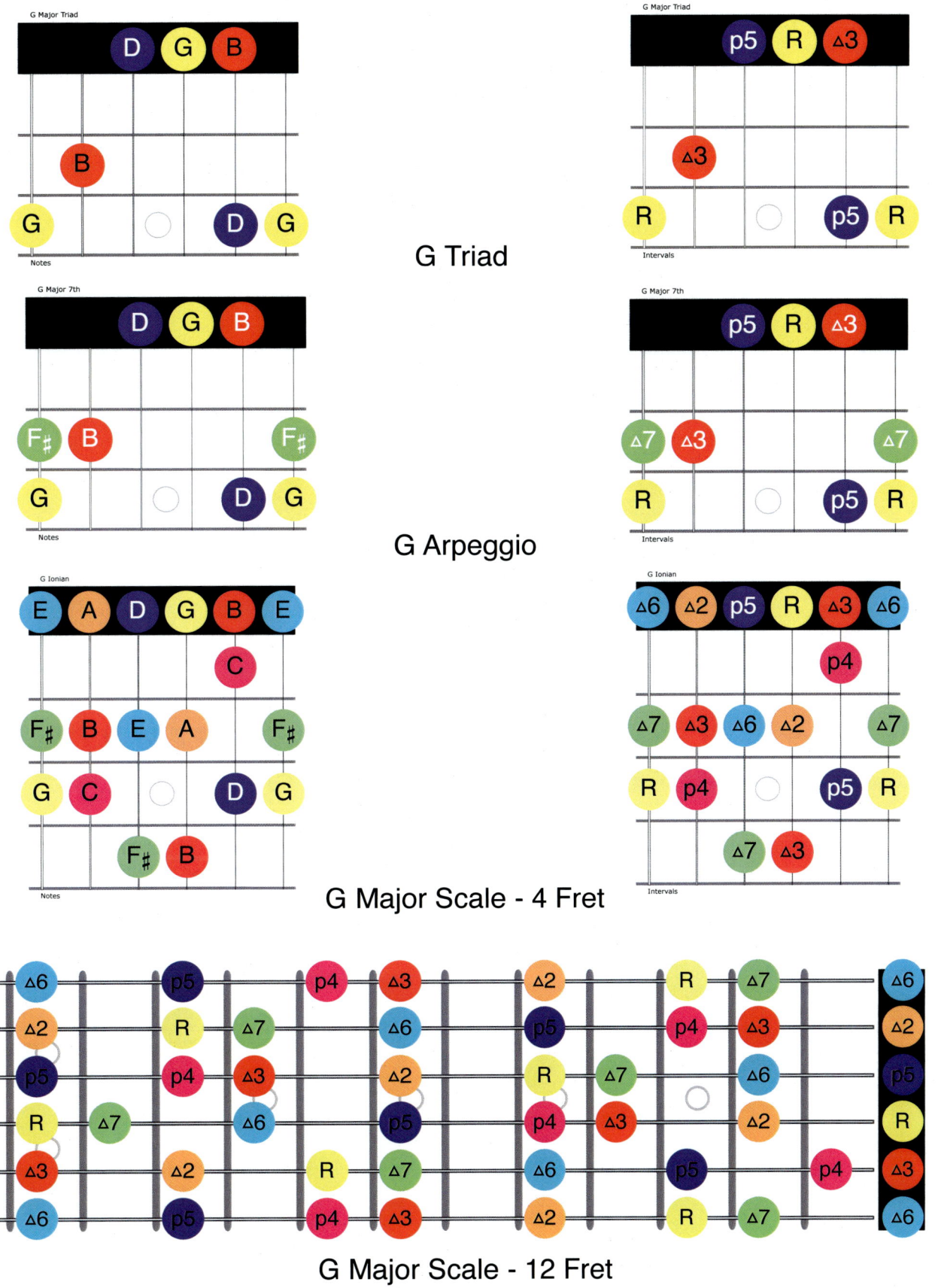

G Triad

G Arpeggio

G Major Scale - 4 Fret

G Major Scale - 12 Fret

Fig. 68. G Major Key - representation of fretboard with notes and intervals.

8 o'clock position
Ab Major Scale - Chromatic Orientation

Ab Major Key
Number of Sharps/Flats = 4 Flats (Bb / Eb / Ab / Db)
Ab - Bb - C - Db - Eb - F - G - Ab
1 - 2 - 3 - 4 - 5 - 6 - 7 - 8
Ab - G - AF- Eb - Db - C - Bb - Ab

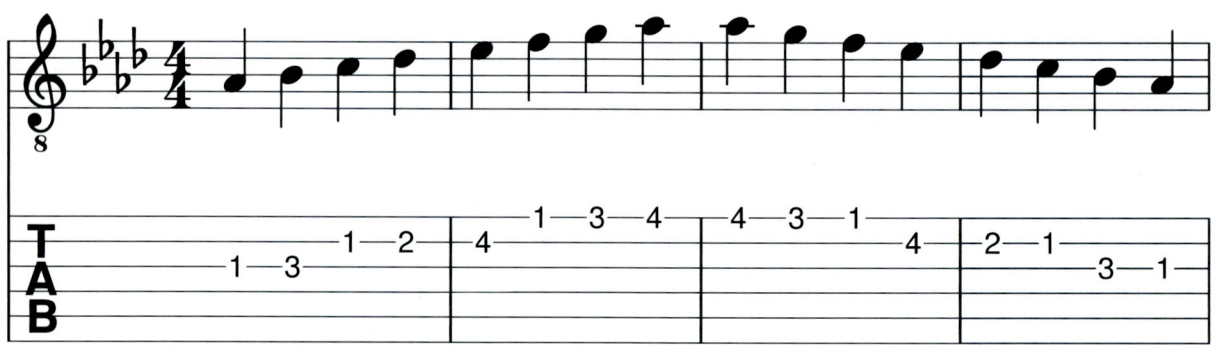

Fig. 69. Ab Major Key viewed in multiple formats - graphic, alphanumerics, staff/tab.

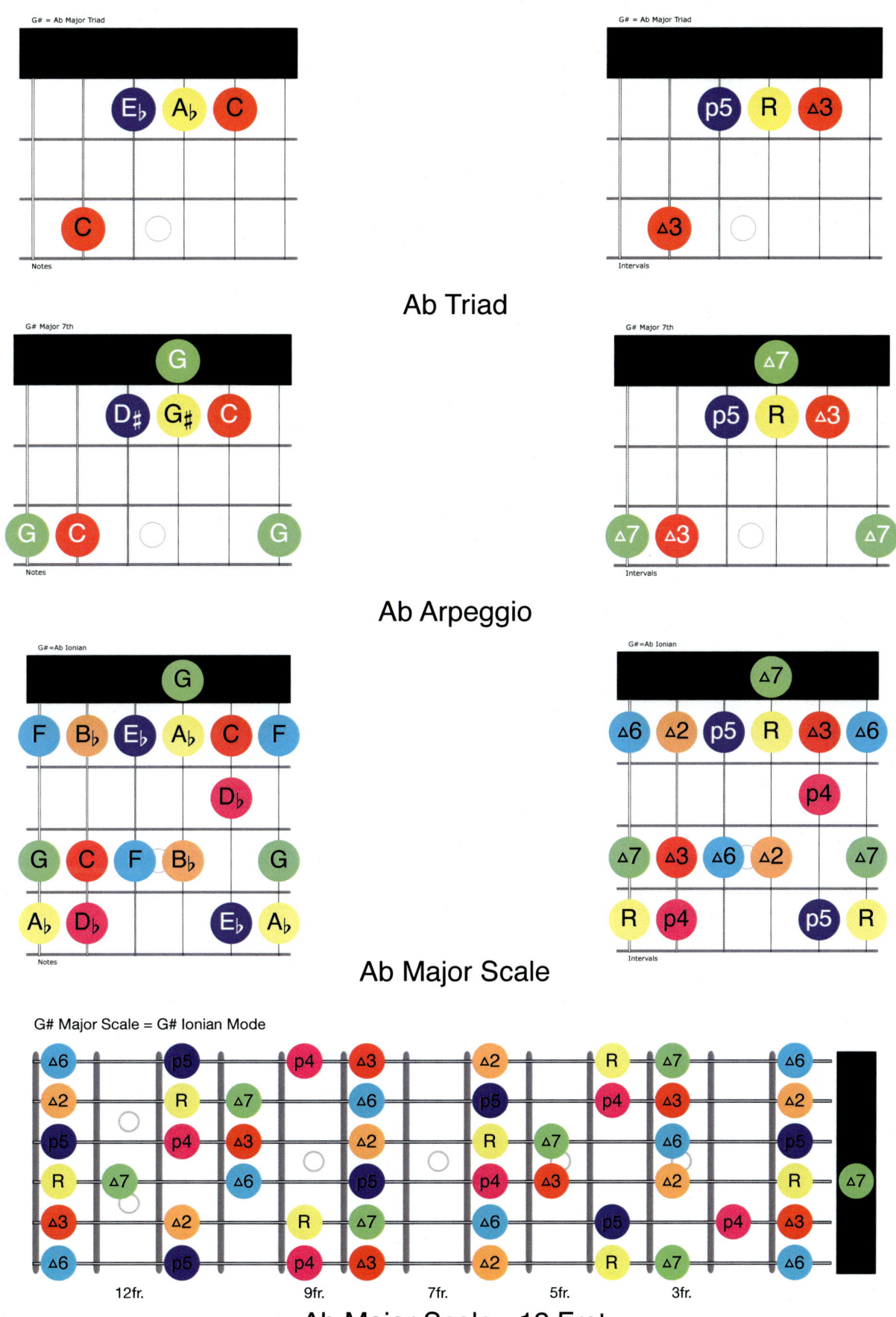

Ab Triad

Ab Arpeggio

Ab Major Scale

Ab Major Scale - 12 Fret

Fig. 70. Ab Major Ke - representation of fretboard with notes and intervals.

A Major Scale - Chromatic Orientation

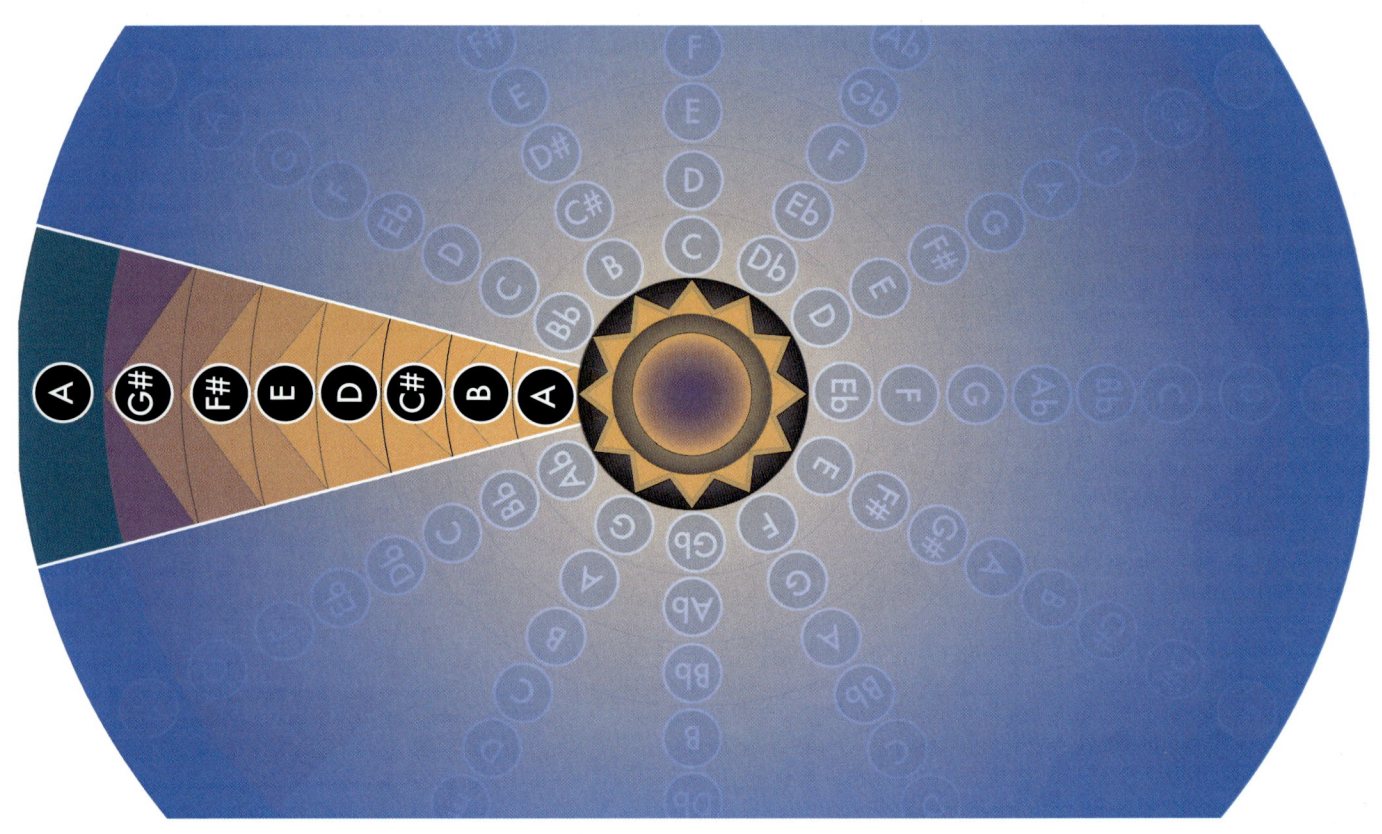

A Major Key
Number of Sharps/Flats = 3 Sharps (F# / C# / G#)
A - B - C# - D - E - F# - G# - G - A
1 - 2 - 3 - 4 - 5 - 6 - 7 - 8
A - G - G# - F# - E - D - C# - B - A

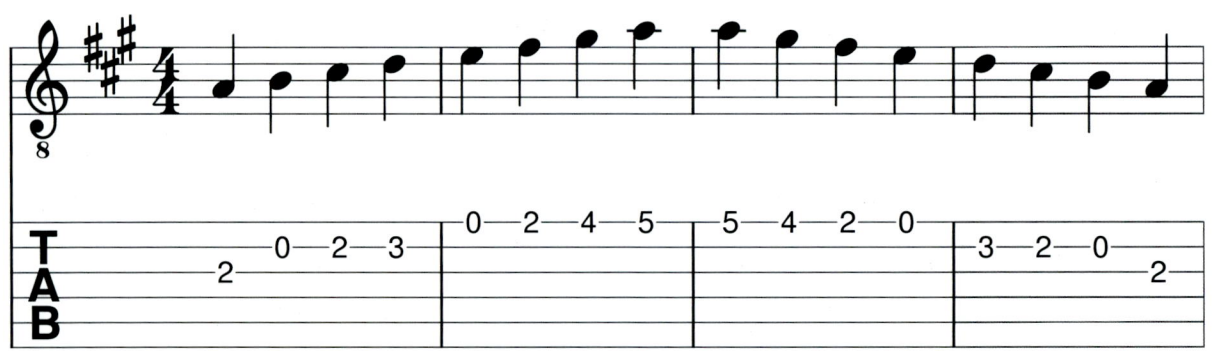

Fig. 71. A Major Key viewed in multiple formats - graphic, alphanumerics, staff / tab.

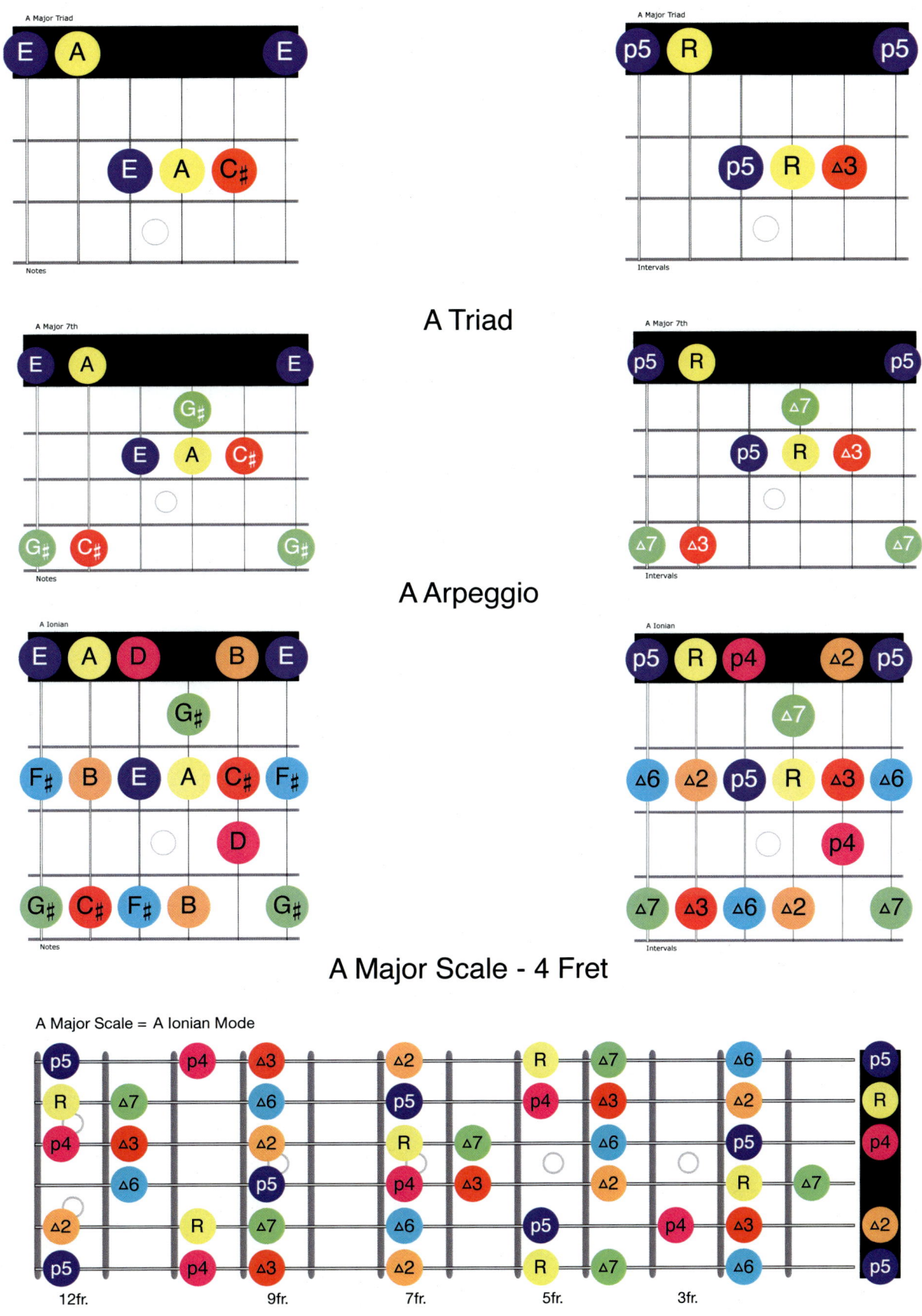

A Triad

A Arpeggio

A Major Scale - 4 Fret

A Major Scale - 12 Fret

Fig. 72. A Major Key - representation of fretboard with notes and intervals.

10 o'clock position
Bb Major Scale - Chromatic Orientation

Bb Major Key
Number of Sharps/Flats = 2 Flats (Bb / Eb)
Bb - C - D - Eb - F - G - A - Bb
1 - 2 - 3 - 4 - 5 - 6 - 7 - 8
Bb - A - G - F - Eb - D - C - Bb

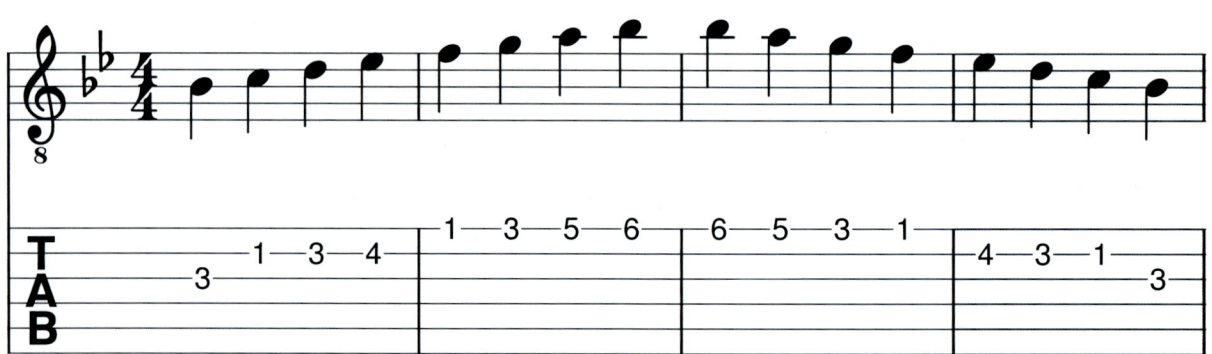

Fig. 73. Bb Major Key viewed in multiple formats - graphic, alphanumerics, staff/tab.

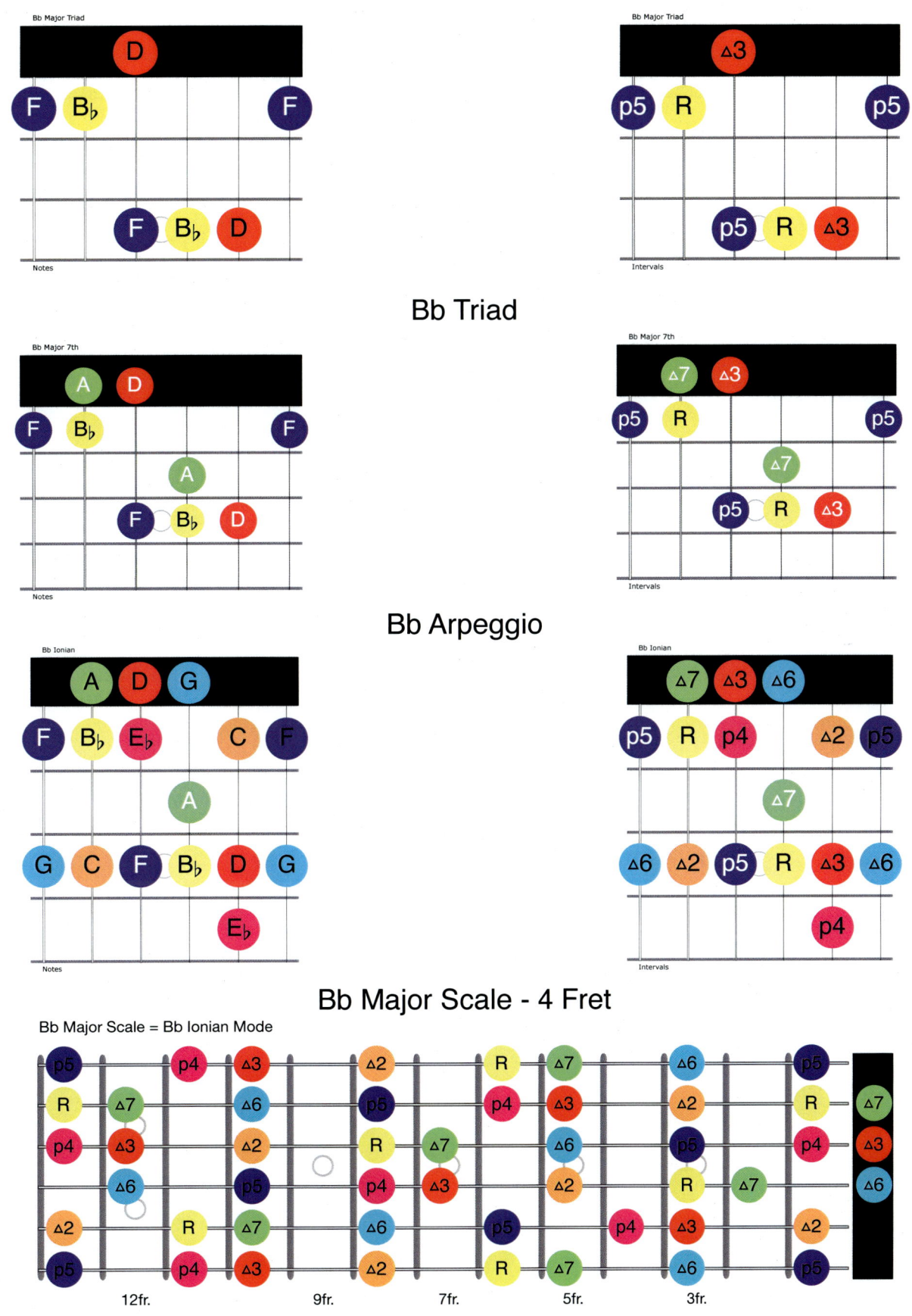

Bb Triad

Bb Arpeggio

Bb Major Scale - 4 Fret

Bb Major Scale - 12 Fret

Fig. 74. Bb Major Key - representation of fretboard with notes and intervals.

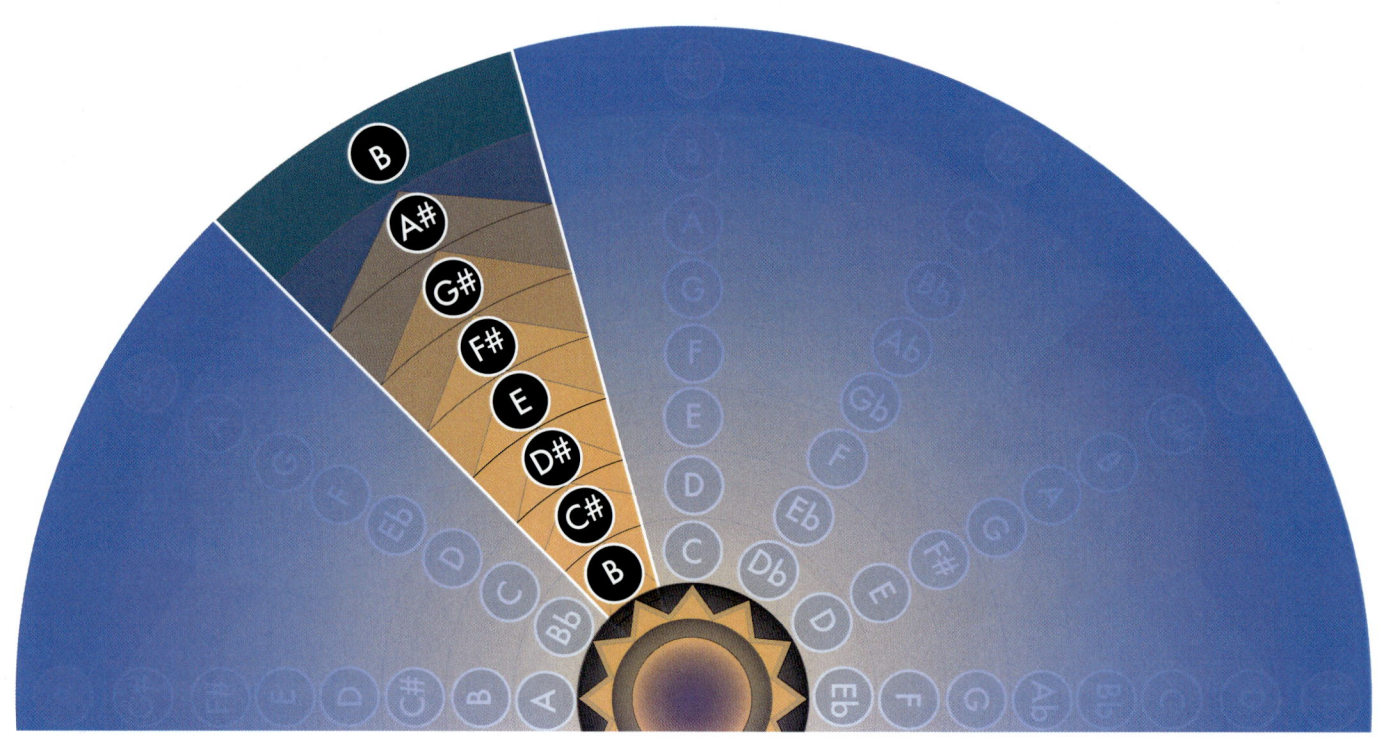

B Major Key
Number of Sharps/Flats = 5 Sharps (F# / C# / G# / D# / A#)
B - C# - D# - E - F# - G# - A# - B
1 - 2 - 3 - 4 - 5 - 6 - 7 - 8
B - A# - G# - F# - E - D# - C# - B

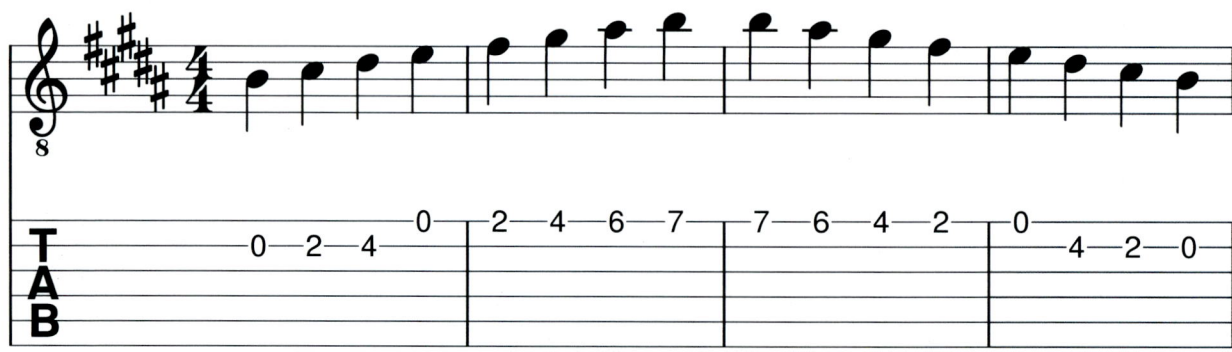

Fig. 75. B Major Key viewed in multiple formats - graphic, alphanumerics, staff/tab.

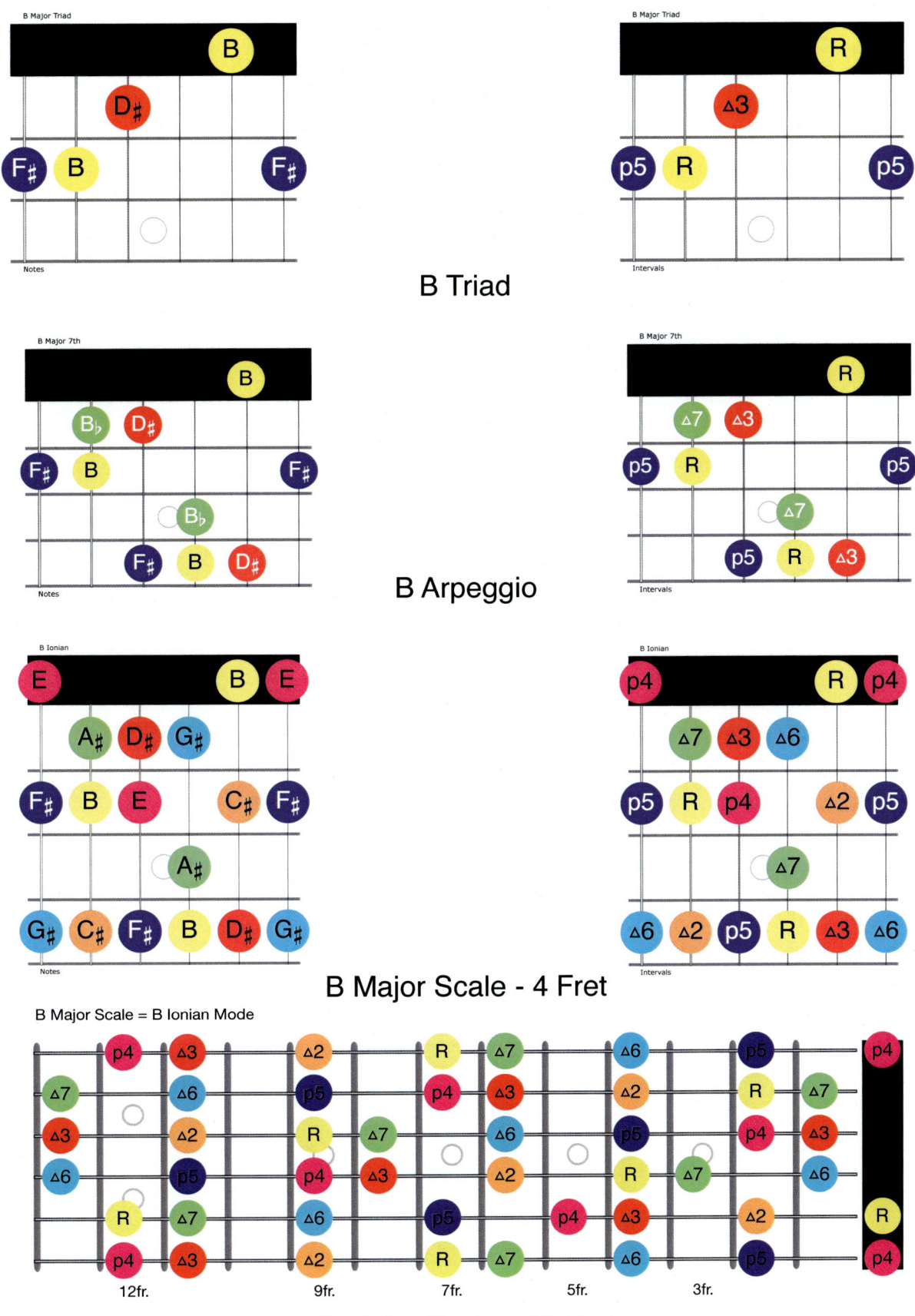

B Triad

B Arpeggio

B Major Scale - 4 Fret

B Major Scale - 12 Fret

Fig.76. B Major Key - representation of fretboard with notes and intervals.

12 o'clock position
C Major Scale - Octave - Chromatic Orientation

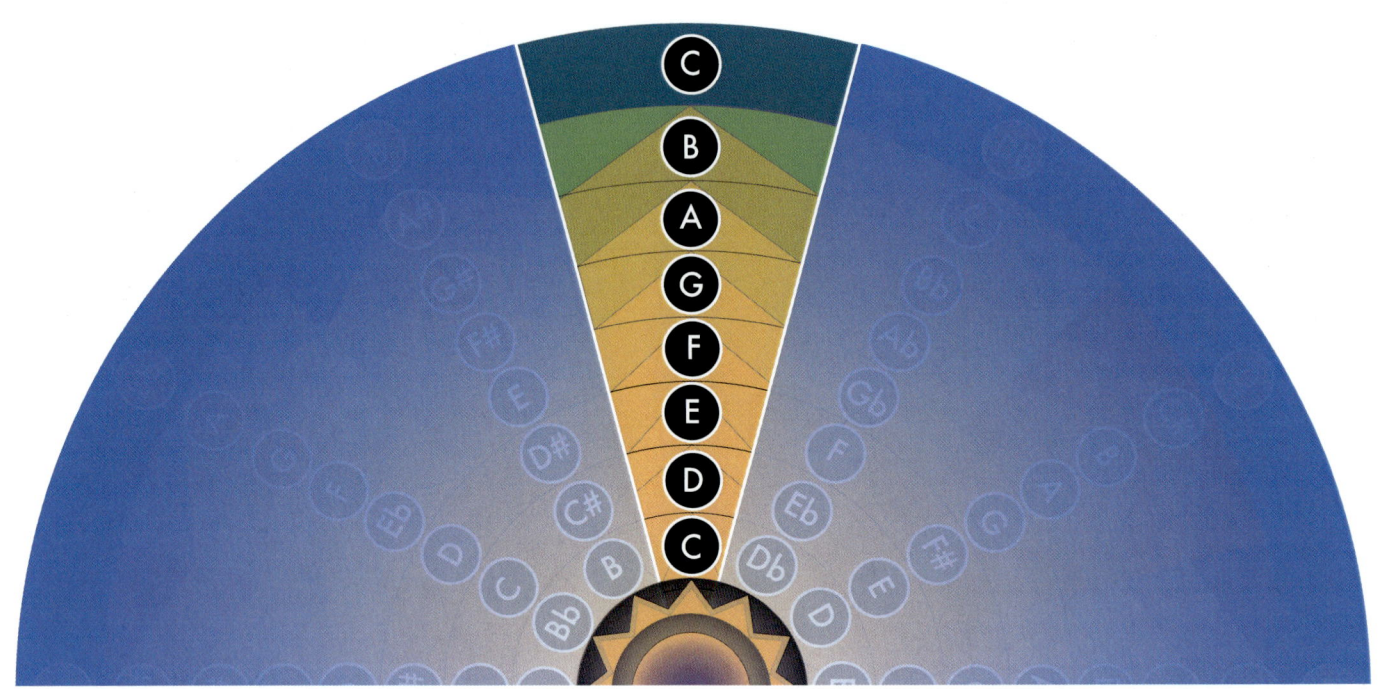

C Major Key
Number of Sharps/Flats = 0 (no Flats / no Sharps)
C - D - E - F - G - A - B - C
1 - 2 - 3 - 4 - 5 - 6 - 7 - 8
C - B - A - G - F - E - D - C

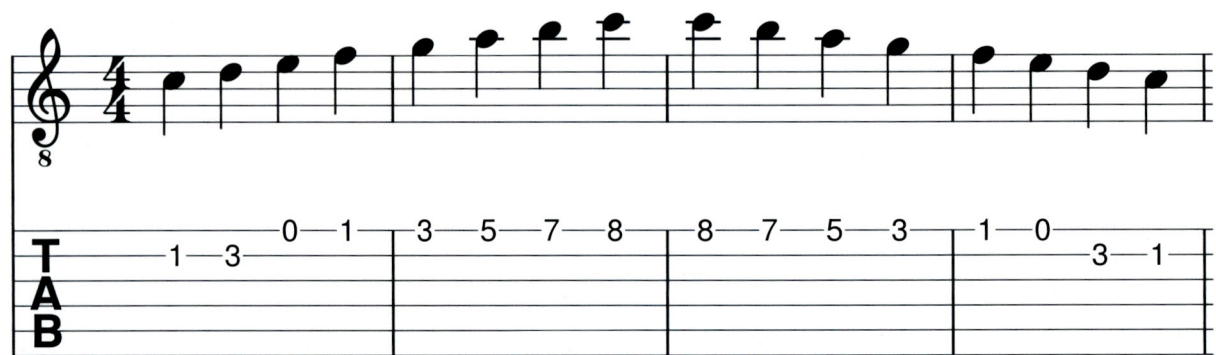

Fig. 77. C Major Key - Octave - viewed in multiple formats - graphic, alphanumerics, staff / tab.

Chords Forming the Harmonized Scale

The following image identifies the seven notes and the corresponding numbers in each slice composing the major scale. The following sequence demonstrates the harmonized scale pattern using the minor chords for the more audibly pleasing effect. This C major scale is the basis of this exercise. These images identify the minor chords, which are essential for the harmonized scale. These minors chords fit perfectly into the harmonized scale pattern. Use these minor chords as adjustments, which are much more pleasing to the ear, rather than using all major chords in the pattern.

Use these minors to fit into the harmonized scale: D minor, E minor, A minor, B(diminished) (Bm7b5).

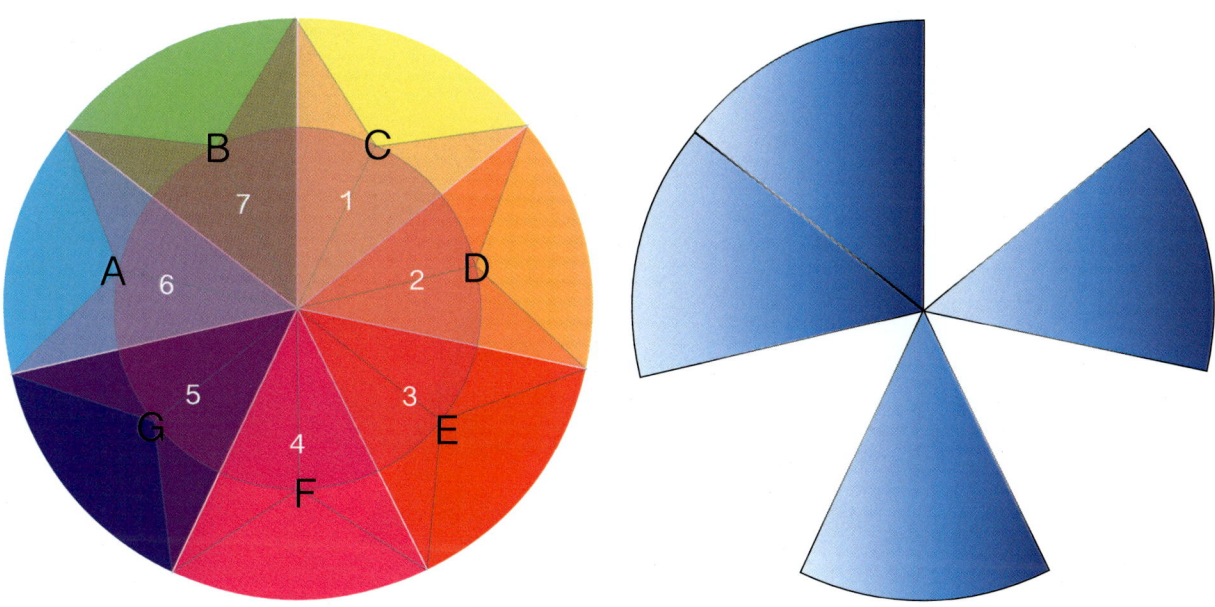

Fig. 78.This wheel provides the correlation of numbers and note names - displayed in the order of the major scale. The stencil on he right will rotate in the following pages unveiling the C harmonized major scale = Magically!

C Basic Triad - Root - Tonic - 1 - 3 - 5 = C - E - G

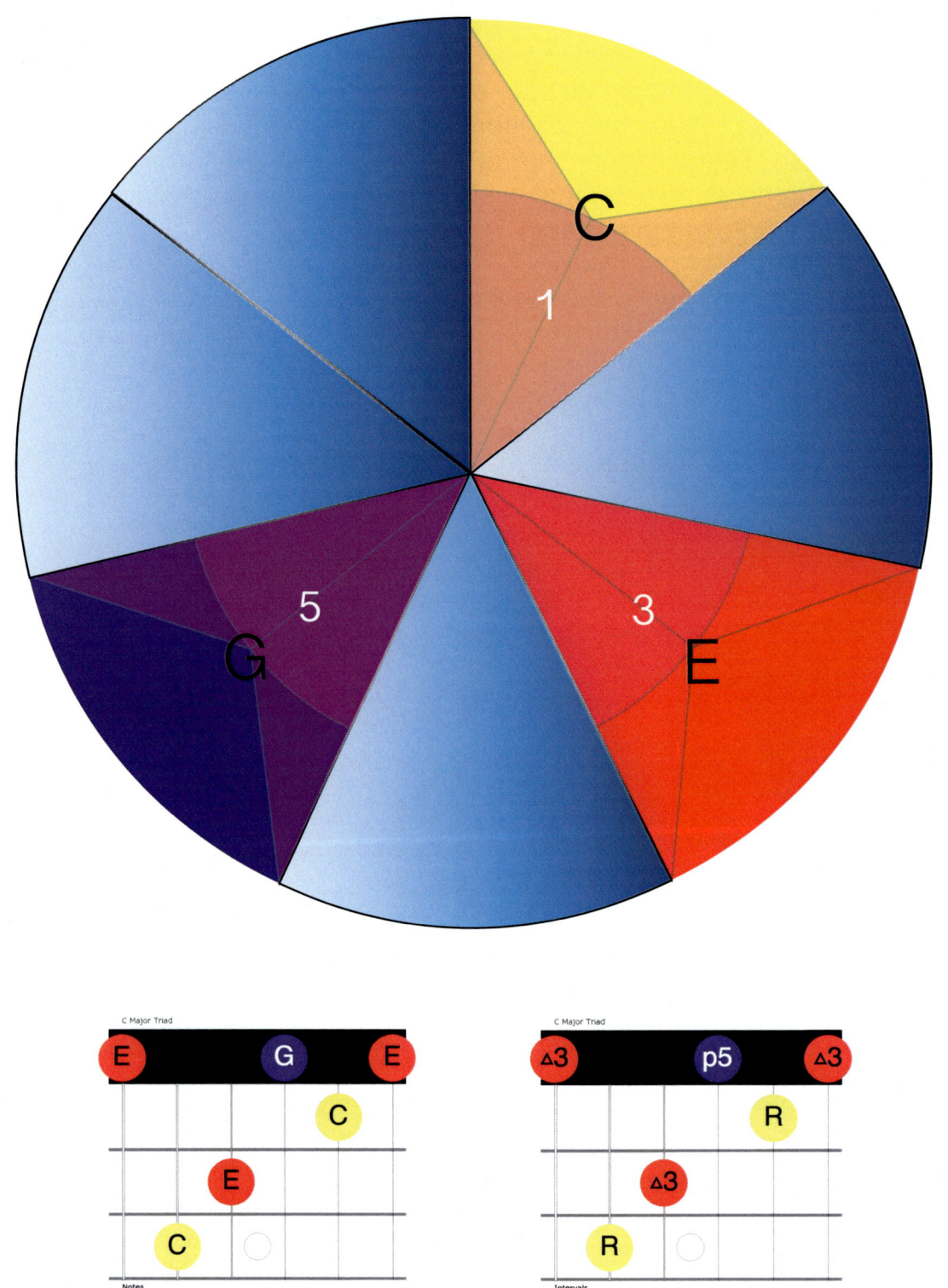

Fig. 79. Stencil blocks unwanted notes resulting in the C basic triad - numbers, notes and intervals. Fingering patterns displayed in notes and intervals.

D Minor Triad - The Two Minor - 2 - 4 - 6 = D - F - A

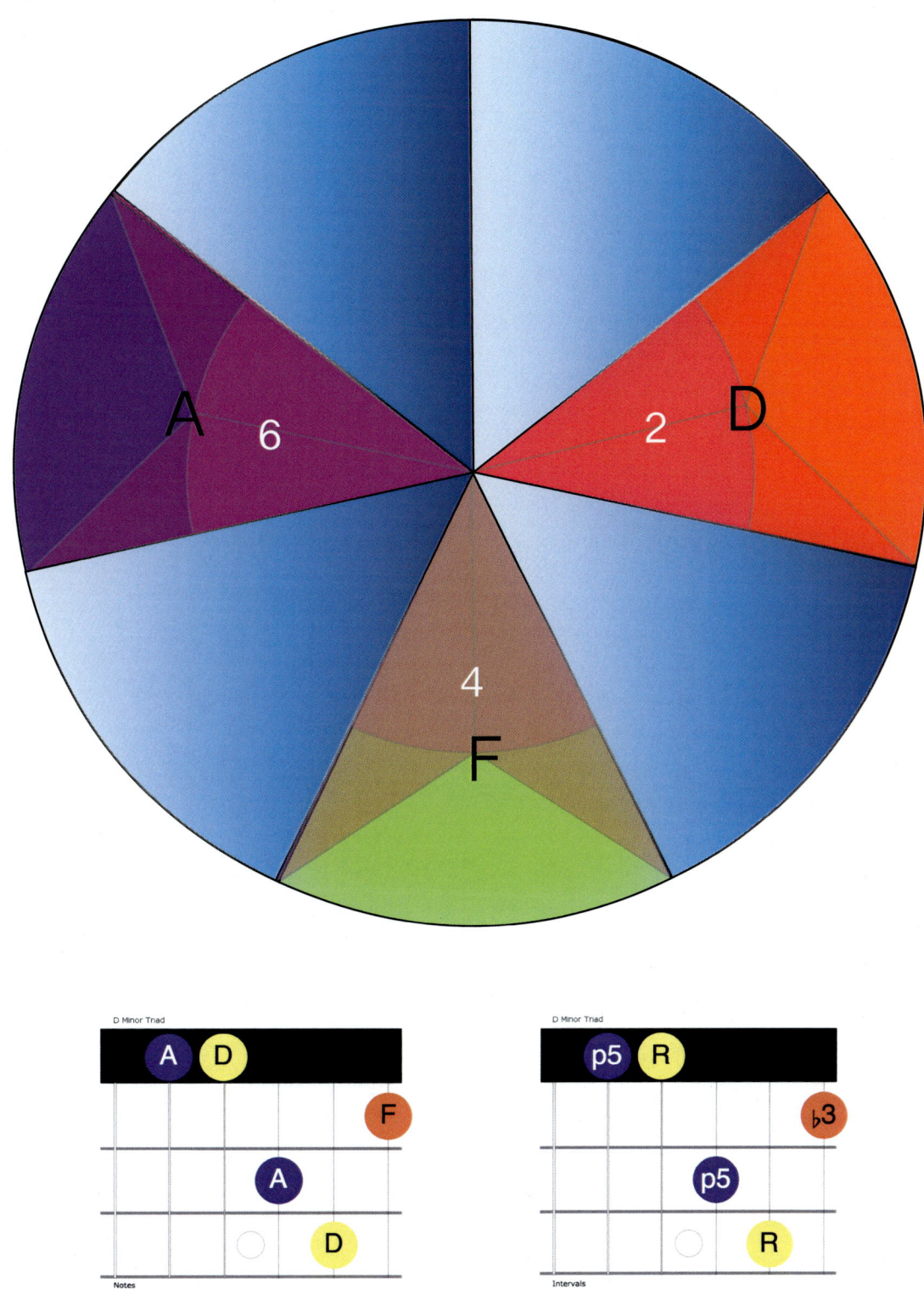

Fig. 80. Stencil blocks unwanted notes resulting in the Dm triad - numbers, notes and intervals. Fingering patterns displayed in notes and intervals.

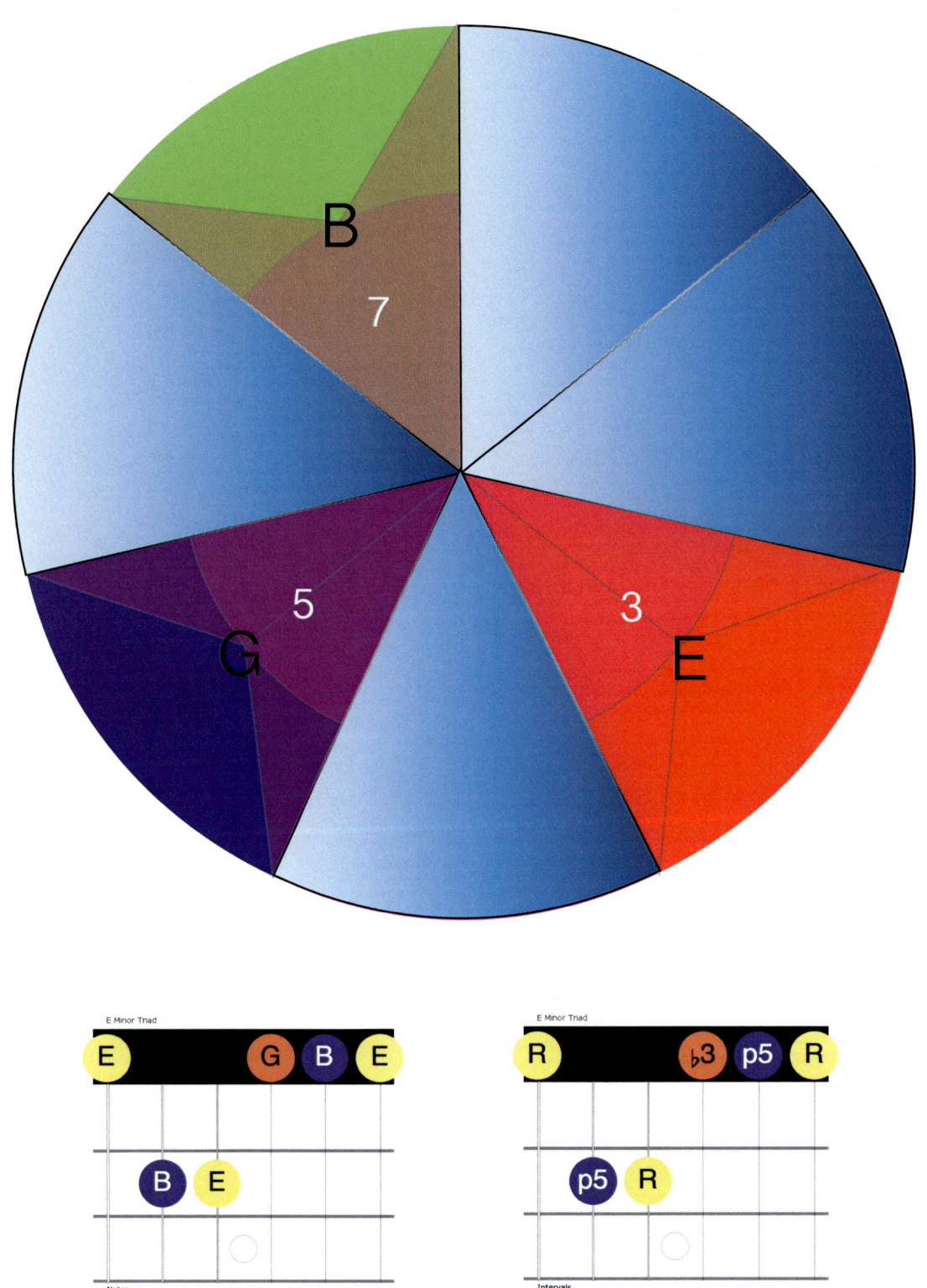

Fig. 81. Stencil blocks unwanted notes resulting in the E minor triad - numbers, notes and intervals. Fingering patterns displayed in notes and intervals.

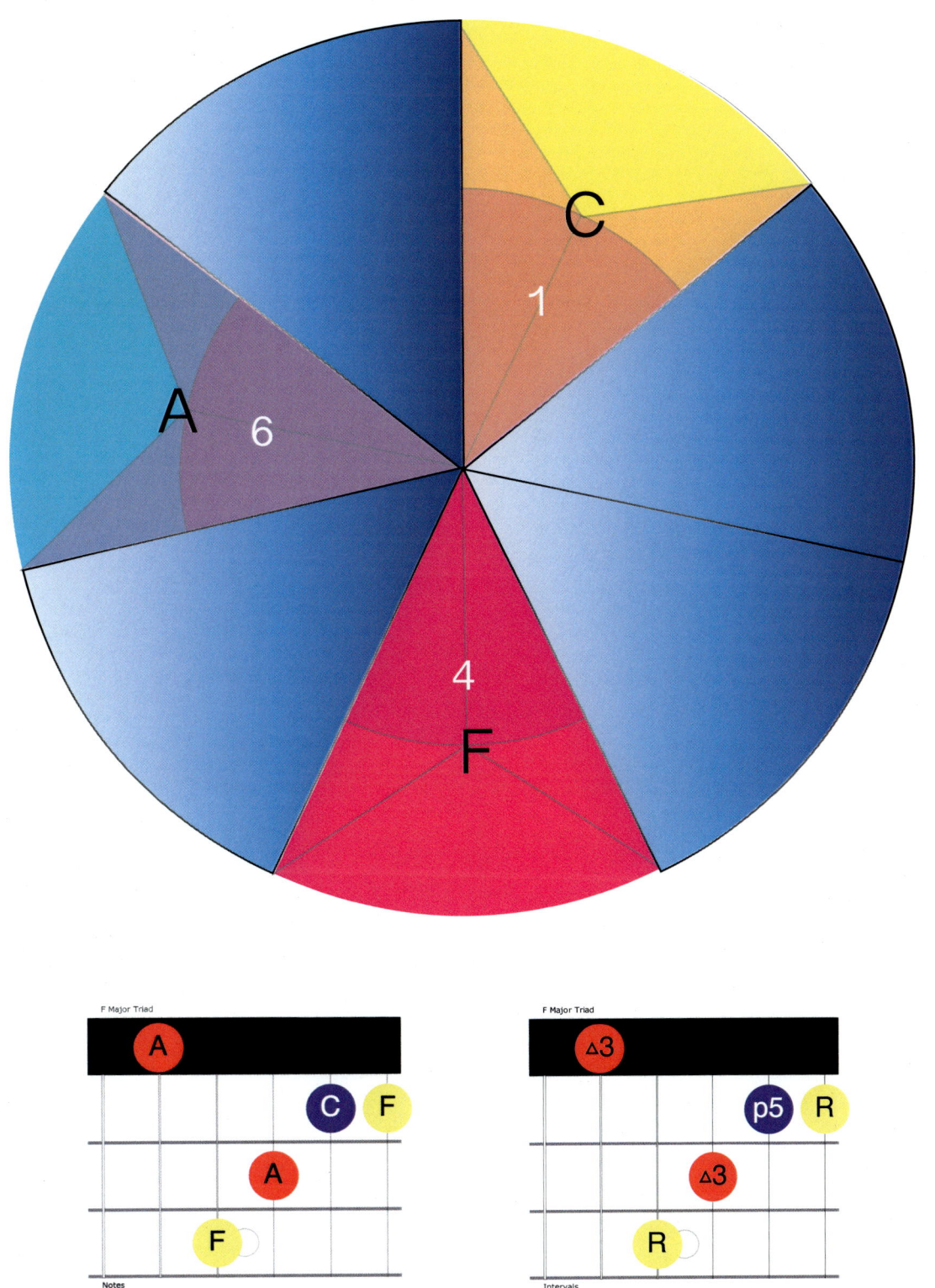

Fig. 82. Stencil blocks unwanted notes resulting in the F major triad - numbers, notes and intervals. Fingering patterns displayed in notes and intervals.

G Major Triad - The Five - Perfect - 5 - 7 - 2 = G - B - D

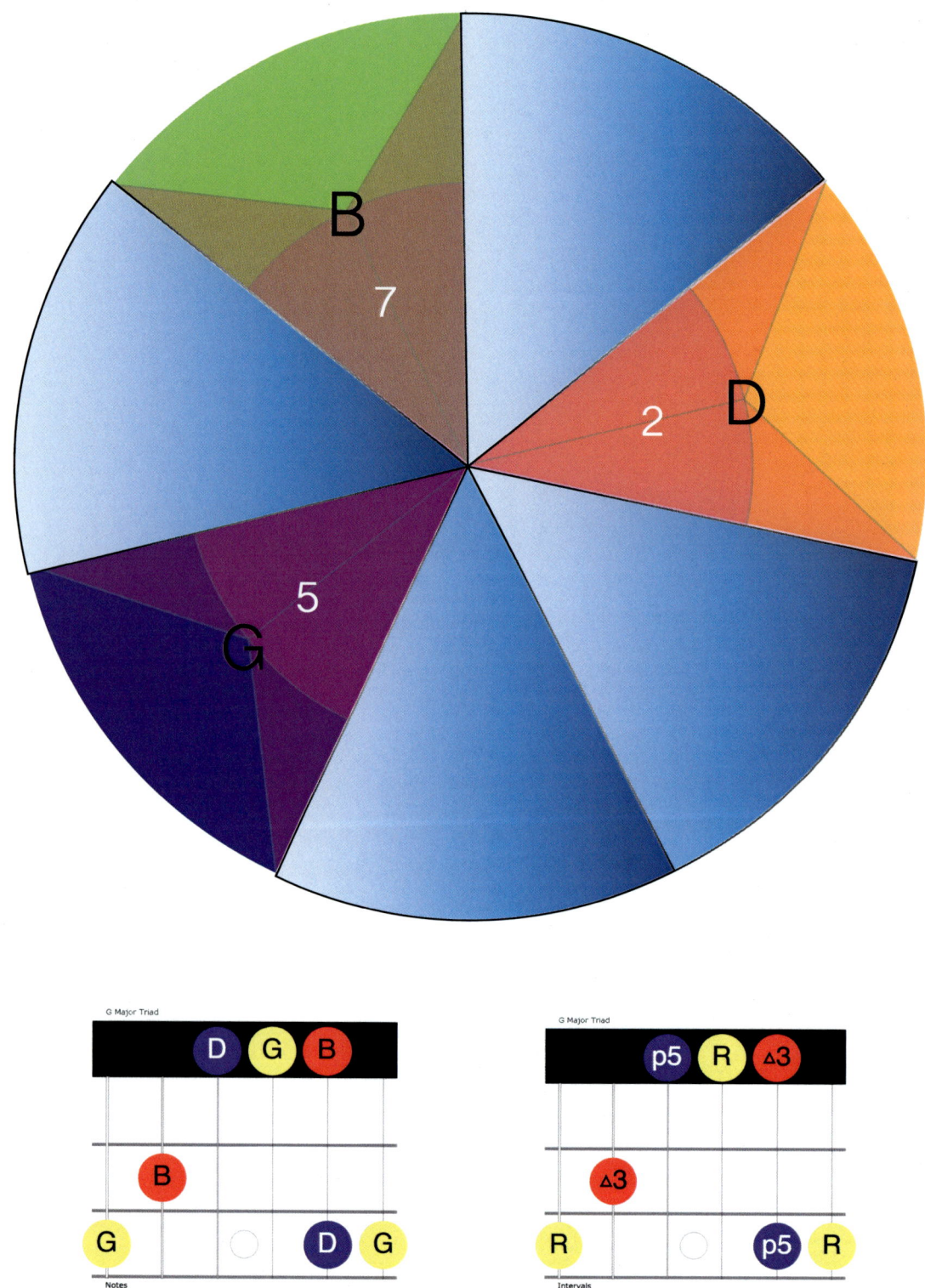

Fig. 83. Stencil blocks unwanted notes resulting in the G major triad - numbers, notes and intervals. Fingering patterns displayed in notes and intervals.

A Minor Triad - The Six - 6 - 1 - 3 = A - C - E

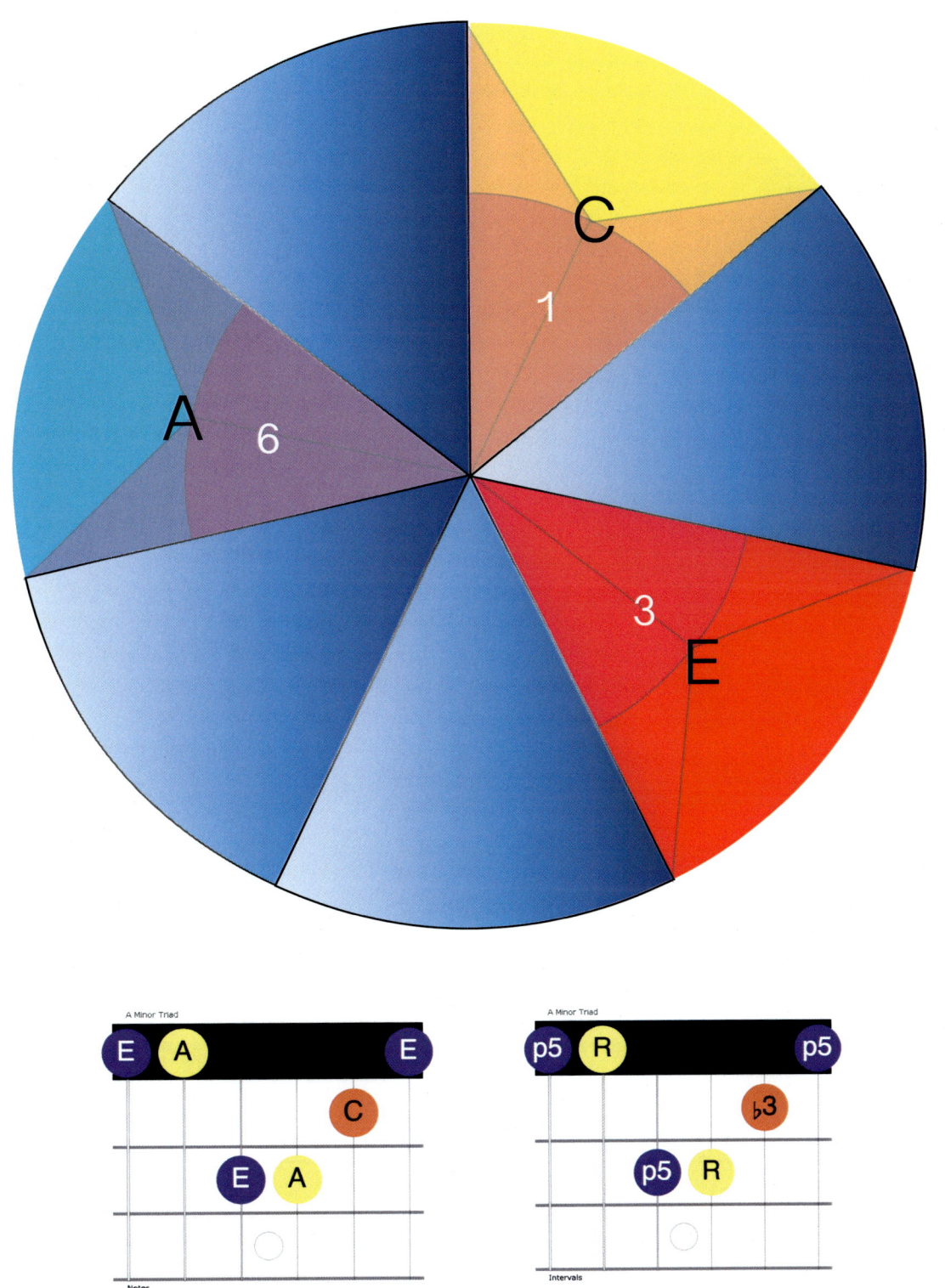

Fig. 84. Stencil blocks unwanted notes resulting in the A minor triad - numbers, notes and intervals. Fingering patterns displayed in notes and intervals.

B Diminished - The Minor7 b5 - 7 - 2 - 4 = B - D - F

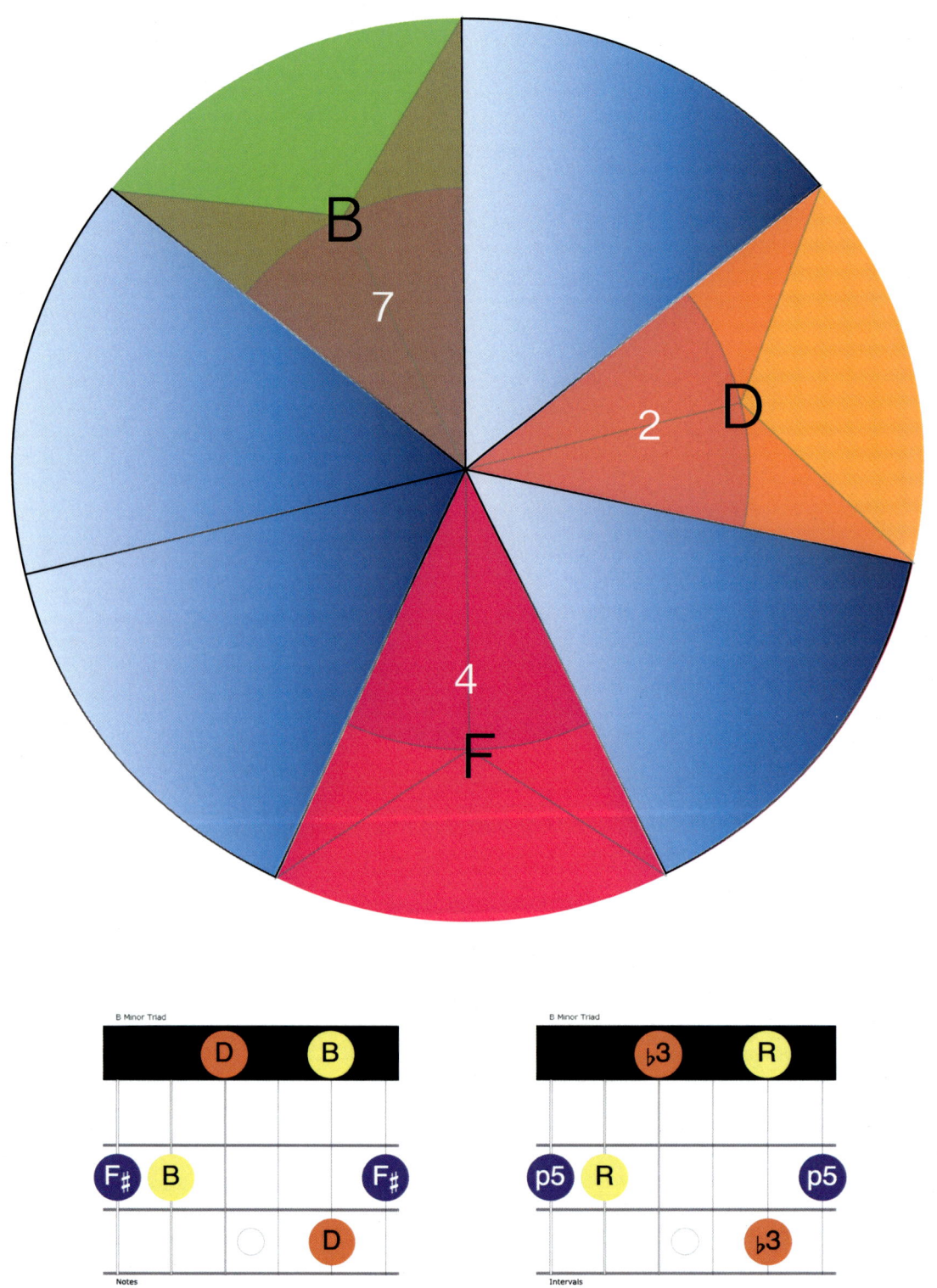

Fig. 85. Stencil blocks unwanted notes resulting in the C basic triad - notes and intervals. Fingering patterns displayed in notes and intervals.

Numbers in Progressions

English	Roman Numerals	Numbers / Integers	Letters in C
One—Four—Five	I — IV — V	1 — 4 — 5	C — F — G
One—Six—Four—Five	I — VI — IV — V	1 — 6 — 4 — 5	C — A — F — G
Two—Five—One	II — V — I	2 — 5 — 1	D — G — C
Six—Two—Five—One	VI — II —V — I	6 — 2 — 5 — 1	A — D —G — C
Two—Five—Seven	II — V — VII	2 — 5 — 7	D — G — B

Fig. 86. Progressions are combinations, sequences and arrangements of chords. Progressions are the backbone and structure of songs and compositions. Progressions have patterns, as do scales and chords. All have distinct functions and relationships. Chords are bound together, forming progressions and compositions. This is a place to start and gain information about a few progressions and patterns to play.

One - Four - Five is a basic and common progression pattern found in the blues = E - A - B; country = C - F - G or G - C - D; and pop = A - D - E.

Two-Five-One * Two-Five-Seven * Two-Six-Five-One * One-Six-Four-Five are additional starting points for playing progressions. These help to unveil patterns for one's own compositions and songs.

The graphic on the next page is based on the "order of sub dominants." Each chord to the right is the fourth degree above. Play the chords in the exact order.

Using the chord diagrams from the previous pages, start with the Bm (Bm7b5) (diminished) = the harmonic seventh degree with a flatted fifth in the key of C, and move straight through this sequence of numbers (letters) from left to right–stop at the "ONE" (the C); (Bm7b5 - Em - Am - Dm - G - C).

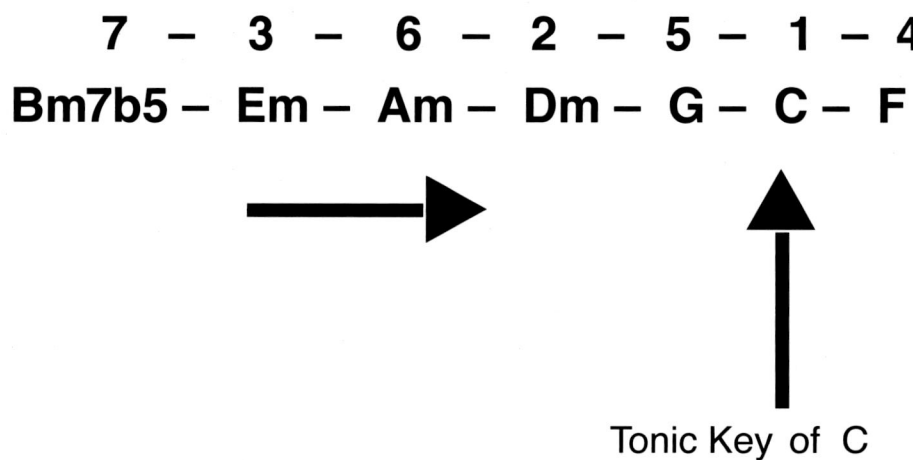

Tonic Key of C

Employ the major chords, when using these degrees of the major scale 1 - 4 - 5. Employ the minor chords, when using the degrees of the major scale = 7 - 3 - 6 - 2.

Notice the number sequence above the chord names; these identify a valuable chord relationship and order, known as the "order of sub-dominants," or the "circle of fourths."

Start with the 1 = C. Count from the 1 (C) left– until you reach the number 7 (Bm7b5). Move from there to the right one chord at a time to the 3 (E minor); from the C to the Em is the third degree of the major scale (**C**-D-**E**), the *secondary relative minor*. Move from there to the right–one chord and arrive at the sixth–*the relative minor*. Next is the Dm, the "second" and a minor chord in the harmonized scale pattern. Last is the G, the dominant, the (fifth) and it resolves to the C.

The four is the F and sub dominant and is perfect. It is also to the right of the Tonic Key C.

An interesting observation about the diagram above is: while moving from the right to the left: C to G to D to A to E to B, the key signatures follow a pattern that increases the number of sharps incrementally, each time by one. And by moving from C to F, the number of flats is increased as well, from zero to one.

This sequential pattern is known as the "order of sub-dominants" or, depending on direction, is also referred to as the "order of dominants."

B - E - A - D - G - C - F - Bb - Eb - Ab - Db - Gb - B

The preceding set of images gives a starting point to make music and play progressions. By adhering to the sequence 1-7, it is the ascending harmonized scale. However, this offers the framework to mix and match and create one's own musical compositions. All the chords fit into a hierarchy and are audibly correct.

Try for fun to create chord progressions using the graphics of the previous page, their corresponding notes and intervals with correct tonal locations.

Summary

In summary, this guide offers an alternative way to visualize, learn and understand the basics and inter workings of music. It is presented with a graphic and progressive approach in mind. The purpose of this effort is to open one's imagination, provide guidance and direction, and aid in the development skills and the understanding of musical principals. This manuscript is for the many musicians looking to express themselves musically through the guitar.

This guide is presented primarily in the Key of C, This provides a template for all the other keys. When one has mastered the basics in C, the transposition—moving from one key to another—is simple, truly extensive and expansive.

This method is for everyone. By using this guide as a tool, one is able to gain the true basics, the foundations and rudiments found in music. This tool emphasizes the conceptual and theoretical aspects of what makes music work, the mechanics, mathematics, and how it all fits together. This is accomplished graphically. This book builds from the simple and progresses to the complex. This method fills in the blanks for those who want to understand and have not had the chance—or the tools and time to use—in the quest for being a better musician. This is a tool for expressing one's own music through improvisation, practice and jamming with others.

This frames the subject matter in a cohesive and progressive presentation.

Acknowledgments

A special thanks to my immediate and extended family, cousins and friends.

*Thank all of you for the support and your unwavering belief in me
and the value of this project.*

"A Toast to Absent Friends"

About the Author

Ben Ryan is a creative spirit, with concentration and focus on music, art, writing and the guitar. He is a technology innovator and inventor with families of U.S. patents. He is a resourceful, multi-disciplined, full-time student of life.

As a musician, he has played since he was seven, including piano, trumpet, voice and guitar.

In the early 1970s he spent nearly a year in New Orleans, experiencing the food, the life and the music scene there. He worked at WYES-TV as a production specialist. He was involved as a producer with a special-feature program highlighting the "Jazz and Heritage Festival." Soon thereafter, he lived in the West Village of New York City. He joined the staff of the world-famous: Cafe Wha?. He made the most of that time with all New York had to offer, friends, food and familiar places such as the coffee houses, art lofts and music studios.

Later on, he spent more than a decade as a pioneer in the burgeoning computer-generated graphics industry. From the very onset working with a General Electric Division, partnering with NASA on the simulated flight and animation program, exclusively for the Apollo Space Program, Mr. Ryan demonstrated and realized management and corporate leadership.

His work has been viewed globally, corporately and governmentally, including a major presentation to the Senate sub-committee on new communications technologies. He was an instrumental leader in the transition of Northrop Aircraft from conventional artwork techniques to the computer-generated methodologies, protocols and processes. Soon after, he started his own successful production company–creating custom graphic solutions and computer generated presentations–long before PowerPoint–in downtown Los Angeles, California with numerous Fortune 500 Companies as clients.

Most recently, he has been involved with the development of patented musical accessories. In addition, he spends his time on the development of new methods for understanding the "big picture": how music theory and the guitar fit together. His writing and Illustrations use visualizations and graphics to illustrate complex concepts simply.

Ben Ryan

The End of Volume 1